PARTNERSHIP IN PARISH

Best wishes, Irene
Enda Lyons
28/11/93

Enda Lyons

Partnership in Parish

A vision for parish life, mission and ministry

the columba press

the columba press

93, The Rise, Mount Merrion, Blackrock, Co. Dublin

Revised edition 1993
First edition 1987
(*seven printings*)

Designed by Bill Bolger
Origination by The Columba Press
Printed in Ireland by
Genprint Ltd, Dublin

ISBN: 1 85607 088 3

Imprimatur:
Joseph Cunnane
Archbishop of Tuam
August 15th 1986

Acknowledgements

Most of the material in this book was worked out over some years with helpful groups and individuals – in Mount Oliver and more recently, in my own archdiocese and in the Pastoral Centres in Donamon and Galway. I am grateful to these for all their comments, stimulation, support and encouragement. I am grateful also to my brothers Albert and Noel, and to Eamonn, for their encouragement after reading the first draft. I am especially indebted to Colm Burke for his careful reading of the manuscript and for his many perceptive and helpful comments. I thank Bishop Michael Murphy of Cork and Ross for permission to quote from his pastoral, *The Parish: the challenge ahead.*

In memory of
my mother and father

For
Pobal Dé
especially of
The Archdiocese of Tuam

Contents

Introduction

This book has been written for all who belong to a parish. It has been written particularly for those in a parish who feel that they do not *really* belong – who feel that they are only 'pupils' there and think that their place is to be always at the receiving-end of the parish's ministry. Its purpose is to remind these that the parish has an important task to perform in their locality, not just for God, but also for the people there – the two causes, God's and people's, are one. Its purpose also is to remind them that, as members of a parish, they have been called – as much as the priest has – to be involved in their parish's task of making their part of the world a better place for young and old to live in, and therefore a better world for God, because it is in such a situation that God reigns.

This book does not set out to describe the parish as it is. It presents rather a vision for what a parish might be and what, I think, it is meant to be The vision, I believe, is one which challenges – but any vision for a Christian community must be such.

The book can be read privately or with a view to group discussion. I would hope that parish groups especially would find it a useful basis for discussion and a help for pastoral planning.

Enda Lyons
August 15th 1986

1

Chapter One
The parish – people

The best way to begin talking about partners in parish is to ask what is a parish. This, of course, is something about which almost everyone has some knowledge. A person does not have to be very well informed about Church matters to know, for example, that the word 'parish' refers to a unit within the Church – a rather self-contained unit. Wherever there are Christians, among whom there is a priest who is responsible for their pastoral care, there we have what, in an English dictionary at least, would be called a parish. In this book I shall use the word 'parish', in this perhaps rather loose sense, to refer to the Christian community as it exists in a particular locality – in other words, to a 'local Church'.

Since I am using the word 'parish' to refer to a local *Church*, there is only one way to find out what a parish is – that is, to find out what the Church itself is.

The Church Today
The Church exists now for almost 2,000 years. Over the centuries it has, inevitably perhaps, become a highly structured, complex organisation. It has its *office-holders* – deacons, priests, bishops, Pope. It has its *worship* – Mass, sacraments, rituals, blessings. It has its *holy things* – oil, water, ashes, palms. It has its *holy times* – Sunday, feast days, fast days, Advent, Christmas, Lent, Easter, Pentecost. It has its *holy places* – basilicas, cathed-

rals, churches, shrines. It has its *teachings* – creeds, dogmas, doctrines, catechisms. It has its *discipline* – commandments, rules, regulations and rubrics. It has a *bureaucratic element* at every level of its existence – Vatican, national, diocesan, even parish. The Church is such a complex and complicated organisation today that it can be easy, even for one of its own members, to be so distracted by the details as to forget what these are all about. To understand what the Church really is, we must get behind these complicated structures and remember again what is at the heart of it all.

A good way to do that is to recall some elementary, but very important, facts about how the Church came to be in the first place (a way followed by James P Mackey, *The Church: its credibility today*, Bruce, New York, 1970, ch 2). I say *some* elementary facts, because the question of the origin of the Church is itself a very interesting one about which scholars have a lot to say. However, many aspects of the question, interesting and important as they are, do not concern us here.

How the Church came to be – one story
Most Catholics are not very conscious of having a story about how the Church came to be. Still, at the back of their minds they have their own version of what happened and even though they may not be aware of it, their story has a profound influence on their understanding of what the Church is.

The following, I think, is a fairly accurate account of their story. They would think of the Church as coming to be in two stages. The *first* stage would have to do with an organisation. They would think of Jesus of Nazareth as first setting up an organisation: they would think of him, for example, as teaching certain truths which people were to believe, laying down certain laws which they were to follow, instituting certain sacraments which they were to receive or celebrate, and appointing certain authority-figures whom they were to obey. The *second* stage would have to do with people: they would see Jesus as then inviting or commanding people to join the organisation. In this version of the story, organisation or 'things' come first and people second.

Comment
Two points in particular might be made about this account of the Church's origin.

The first is that, obviously, there is a lot of truth in it. There is, and always was, an organisational side to the Church – there are definite beliefs to be held, sacraments to be celebrated, leaders to be followed, and so on. Furthermore, these owe their origin in some way to Jesus – though how *precisely* each of them can be traced back to Jesus is one of the questions which scholars discuss.

The second comment is that this version of the story, despite the truth which it contains, can be a misleading one. It can leave us with a very distorted picture, not just of how the Church came to be, but of what it *is*. Consequently, it can leave us with a wrong notion of what a parish is. We shall see this if we consider the Church as a *human community*.

The Church as a human community
No Christian, I think, would say that the Church is *merely* a human community, no different from any other one. Every Christian knows that there is more to the Church than meets the eye. The Church, for ex-

ample, is of divine origin – the first step in its formation was taken by God, not by people. Those who make up the Church are a people who are *called* by God – indeed this idea of 'call' is the key-idea expressed in the Hebrew, Greek and Latin words for 'church'. The Church also has an inner spiritual life. It is because there are these and other sides and depths to the Church that we can speak of it in terms such as 'The Body of Christ' and as a 'Spirit-filled' community. And it is for this reason too that the Second Vatican Council began its main document on the Church by talking about 'The Mystery of the Church'. Admittedly, it may not always be clear to everyone what precisely some of these descriptions of the Church mean. But this much is clear: they are ways of saying that there is a depth-dimension to the Church which makes it more than an ordinary, everyday human community or society. If we were to lose sight of this, we would have a very superficial idea of what the Church really is and, indeed, of what a parish really is.

But true and important as this is, another point has to be remembered also. To say that the Church is *more* than an ordinary human community does not mean it *ceases* to be one. The Church still has all the elements of a human community and, in its coming-to-be, it followed the basic familiar pattern of the coming-to-be of human communities and societies generally. So, if we reflect on the way in which other communities around us come to be, we shall see something very important – admittedly not everything which is important – about how the Church came to be. More relevant to our purposes in this book, we shall see something very important about what the Church *is*.

How communities come to be

If we think about it, we shall see that, in coming into existence, every community or society goes through three main stages or phases.

The first is that of *interest*. As the word implies, this is the stage when people become interested in something – and interest which, as we shall see, is going to be the basis of the future community or society. Without this interest, there would never be any human association of any kind. For example, unless there was interest in tennis there would be no such thing as a tennis club, and unless there was interest in learning there would be no such thing as school.

The second stage is that of *association*. People who are interested in something, naturally and spontaneously seek out and associate with others who have the same interest. They do this so as to share their interest with others and to be of mutual help in pursuing it. Again, if this did not happen, there would never be a community or society or club of any kind – for example, there would never be a football association or club if people who are interested in football never associated with one another.

The third stage is that of *organisation*. When people who share a common interest associate with one another for the purpose of sharing and pursuing their interest, they automatically set up, or avail of, whatever structures or institutions they think will help them to pursue their interest. For example, they will form a committee and appoint people – like a treasurer and a secretary – who are willing to take on various services for the group. If their interest is tennis, they will go about providing courts and a club-house which will make it possible for them to play and enjoy tennis.

7

They will also agree on whatever rules are necessary to help the members to pursue their interest in tennis.

Structures
I ought to emphasise two points in particular about these organisational or structural elements in a community or association.

The first is that structures are not there for their own sake: they are not an end in themselves. They are at the service of that element which constituted the first stage of the coming-to-be of the community, that is, the *interest* which the people have in common, whether it be tennis, football, bridge, farming or whatever. If they do not facilitate the pursuit of this *interest*, they serve no useful purpose in the community.

The second is a related point. Granted that these structures – the tennis courts, the committee, the rules – are necessary if the association is to survive, still the structures themselves will survive only if, and only as long as, the basic element, the *interest*, survives. If people's interest in tennis were to cease, grass would very soon be growing on even the finest of hard courts, and even the most efficient committee would soon have to disband. The first element, the *interest*, always remains the basic one in every community or society.

The coming-to-be of the Church
The above considerations have something to teach us about the Church. Even though we believe it to be of divine origin, nevertheless, in its coming-to-be, the same basic pattern as that outlined was followed.

Central to the Church is, of course, Jesus of Nazareth, the one who lived and died and was raised. From the point of view of those who made up the Church,

8

the first stage in its coming-to-be was their *interest in Jesus*. It would be impossible at this point – indeed even in this book – to give a full account of why they were interested in him. Here it is sufficient to say that what he said and did and stood for, made sense to them, struck deep chords in them – the very deepest chords, in fact – gave meaning and direction to their lives, gave them a new understanding of their life and death and destiny. As James P Mackey puts it, they found that they 'were enriched by their experience of the person, life and fate of Jesus of Nazareth', that their 'spirits were enlarged by his spirit' (*The Church*, page 43). Or, in the words of St John's gospel, they found him to be 'the Way, the Truth and the Life' (14:6). Without this interest in Jesus of Nazareth, the Church would never have come to be.

Inevitably the second stage, that of *association*, had to follow. Even if there had been no other forces at work, the many people whose experience was enriched by Jesus of Nazareth would, quite spontaneously, have felt the need to seek one another's company and to associate with one another. They would have wanted to exchange ideas about Jesus, to pray in his name, to celebrate together the new way in which they found him present among them after the resurrection. So, as James P Mackey says, 'If Jesus had not founded a community, it would quite literally have founded itself' (*The Church*, page 43).

It is within this context that we ought to situate the *organisational* element in the Church: the people who were interested in Jesus of Nazareth would obviously have availed of whatever structures or institutions or 'things' which would help them to understand Jesus better and follow him more faithfully.

What the Church basically is

What I have said tells us something very important, not just about how the Church came to be, but also about *what it is.* Despite its complex and complicated appearance, its many structures, the Church is, in one sense, something very simple. Basically it is *people* – people who are enriched by their experience of Jesus of Nazareth, who associate with others who have the same experience and interest, and who avail of all the means which help them to follow him.

When I say that this is what the Church *basically* is, I do not, as I have already said, intend to imply that that is *all* it is. I mean that everything else is based on this. Here one of the creation stories from the Book of Genesis comes to mind. In one of these stories God is pictured as creating the human person in two stages. He is pictured as first of all fashioning the form and shape of man, as a potter would, out of clay. Then, in the second stage, he is pictured as breathing into that 'a breath of life'. And 'thus', the story goes, 'man became a living being' (Genesis, 2: 7). It is something similar in the case of the Church. The people whose interest in Jesus of Nazareth brings them to associate with one another in a structured way, are 'the clay model' into which the Spirit breathes the breath of life – and thus the Church too becomes the Spirit-filled body which we believe it to be.

We now see what constitutes the basis of the local Church, the parish. In the sense in which I have just explained, this too is basically *people*. It is a community of people – including, of course, at least one who is a priest – in a particular locality who find Jesus to be a light, a guide, a power, a strength, an inspiration, who associate with one another in an organised way, and who avail of all means which help them to come to know him more deeply, and to follow him more closely. Only as long as there are such people in a locality will there be a real Church there – a point which, perhaps, is sometimes forgotten when people are talking about parish renewal today. Parish 'structures' or 'things' or 'activities' like Mass, Confession, Devotions are, of course, necessary to sustain people's interest in Jesus – an interest which, when fully developed, we call 'faith' – and to facilitate their desire to be his followers. But what basically constitutes the parish is, not the structures which the people use, but the people who use them and the interest which they have in Jesus of Nazareth.

Chapter Two
Everything for people

The fact that the Church and the parish are basically people has many important implications. It is with some of these – ones which will turn out to be important for understanding the idea of partnership in the parish – that I shall be dealing in this chapter.

A context for everything
First, what I have said provides us with a context within which we can situate everything else in the parish.

It helps us to situate, for example, all the *teaching and preaching* which goes on in the parish. We can see how this fits in if we think about the origin of the Church's teaching and preaching activity. Consider again those who first made up the Church. In their desire to learn more about Jesus, to exchange ideas about him and to share experiences of him, naturally they *talked* about him. It is within this broad context of *talking about Jesus* that we are to situate what we now know in the Church as its 'teaching and preaching' activity. In broad terms at least, this Church activity originally was a matter of followers of the risen Christ, especially those who could speak with authority, talking about him and his significance for living. In broad and simple terms, that is what it still is, or, at least, ought to be. So, the reason that religious teaching and preaching has a place in parish life is that, through this activity, those who are interested in Jesus of Nazareth are

12

helped to understand more about who he was then and what, as the Risen One, he means for their lives now.

It is within this context too that we ought to see the place of the *dogmas and doctrines* of the Church. The sole purpose of all these is to express and explain some aspect of that enriching truth in which the members of the Church are interested – that is, the truth about Jesus of Nazareth and his implications for living. And their whole value in parish life lies in their ability to do this for the people of the parish. Sadly, they do not always do this very successfully. Ironically, Church dogmas and doctrines, though meant to explain, are often experienced by believers as being almost impossible to understand and as being, therefore, little more than tests of faith. As James P Mackey says:

Instead of asking: what do Christians know? we often find ourselves asking: what are Roman Catholics obliged to believe? Instead of looking at Christian preaching as a sacred inheritance that enables us to stand in personal relationship with God and with our fellow man ... we too often see the articles of the creed as a kind of obstacle course that we have to run in order to gain eternal life (*Life and Grace*, Gill and Son, Dublin, 1966, page 141).

Obviously when Church doctrines are seen by people in this way, they have failed to be for them what they are meant to be. One of the great challenges to teachers and preachers in the Church in every age is to express these truths in contemporary language, related to contemporary experience.

The *New Testament* too is a feature of parish life – for one thing, it has a prominent place in the parish Mass. Its place in the life of the parish follows from, and corresponds to, its place in the life of the Church as a whole. To understand its place, we go back again to the early Christians. It was almost inevitable that early in its history a community which centred around the Risen Christ would commit its experience of him to writing. This it eventually did. The New Testament is a collection of very early and very special written accounts of the first community's experience and understanding of Christ. It would take us too far afield to attempt to say here in what precise way they are special. For our purposes it is enough to say that subsequent generations of Christians have always treasured these documents basically because they have found that they capture in a unique way the spirit of Christ, and offer unique possibilities of becoming attuned to him and to his vision for human life. Christians have treasured them, not so much because they have felt obliged to, as because they have found them to be worth treasuring. These writings are, then, a feature of Church life at every level for the simple reason that, in regard to following Jesus, people have found them – and still find them – to be inspired and inspiring.

The interest which the people of the Church have in Jesus of Nazareth also explains the place of *liturgy* in Church life. In life generally, words – be they spoken or written, or even a combination of both – are never adequate to express our more profound feelings and experiences. To express these, we find ourselves having to resort to symbolic action and gesture. So, when words fail us, we find ourselves 'saying it' with a squeeze of the hand, or with a hug, or with a kiss, or with flowers, or with a gift, or with a ring – or with a combination of these. Indeed the more profound our experience is, the more we find ourselves having to re-

14

sort to this language of symbol and gesture in our efforts to express it. The experience which Christians have of Christ is a most profound and mysterious one. It is so deep and inexpressible that Christians have always used the language of symbol and gesture and ritual in their efforts to communicate it and to express it even to themselves. And this is a tradition which goes back to Jesus himself. Here, very simply, is the basis of the Church's liturgical activity. For example, Christians can read about the Last Supper and can talk and preach about it – and they do all these things. However, they have always found that celebrating it by *doing* again in memory of Jesus what he himself did and what he told them to do in his memory, can give them an insight into his significance which words alone do not give. Indeed, they have found that *doing* it in his memory can do for them what symbols alone are so effective in doing. All symbols have that ability to draw a person beneath the surface of things to their depths. For example, the singing of a National Anthem can draw a person beyond the words and the notes of the tune into all the history and the nationhood which they symbolise. Even in a more profound way, Christians have found that celebrating the liturgy can draw them into the mystery which Christ is. Liturgy too, then, is part of Church and parish life for the same basic reason that everything else is: it has the capacity to bring the people who are interested in Jesus of Nazareth into a deeper union with him.

Everything for people
A second point which follows from the fact that the Church is basically people is that everything in the parish, indeed, everything in the Church – literally every-

15

thing – is for people. This point has been put clearly by Karl Rahner:

> In a chess club, too, the main thing is that chess should be played well, and that masters of the game should be trained there. Everything else, the functionaries, the cash registers, the president, the club meeting and statutes are, indeed, necessary and cannot be abolished; but their true meaning is to serve playing chess. All presiding ministers of the Church, from the Pope and the bishops down to the parish priests and chaplains, exist only so that there may be Christians ... All sermons, all papal decrees, all canon law, all sacred congregations in Rome, all bishops – in short the whole organisation of the Church exists only to assist the true Christian life in the hearts of men. Where this meaning is lost it becomes only man's ridiculous presumption before God (*Grace in Freedom*, Burns & Oates, London, 1969, pages 18-9).

Very often this 'meaning' which Rahner mentions *is* lost and the 'things' in the Church are taken to be there for their own sake. Something like this had happened in regard to the Sabbath among some religious people in Jesus' time. In a later chapter we shall see how Jesus exposed this as being, in Rahner's phrase, 'man's ridiculous presumption before God'. The fact that something like this happened before ought to alert us to the possibility of its happening anywhere, anytime.

The real lights in the parish

From what I have said so far, it follows that the real stars in the parish are those who are the best followers of Christ. Again the example of the chess club illustrates this point. The true stars of a chess club are the good players – not necessarily the president or officers

16

– for, after all, the purpose of the club is playing chess. In the same way the true stars of the parish are those men and women who are best at doing what this community is about – that is, following or striving to follow Jesus of Nazareth. Those who hold office in the parish – mostly priests – may indeed be among these. But if they are, it is not because they hold office, but because they are good followers of Christ – good disciples. Since by far the vast majority in the parish do not hold office in it, we can take it that by far the vast majority of the true stars in the parish are men and women who are living and working in the world. Again, Karl Rahner makes his point very clearly in regard to the Church as a whole:

> The true lights of the Church, those who are most important for the eternal salvation of mankind as well as of individuals are ... those who possess and radiate most faith, hope and love, most humility and unselfishness, most fortitude in carrying the cross, most happiness and confidence. If a Pope does all this as well or perhaps even better than, for example, John XXIII, well, then he is not only a Pope but a wonderful Christian; then it happens that, if I may say so, the president of the chess club is for once also himself a great chess player (*Grace in Freedom*, page 19).

The term 'lay person' in the parish
A third point which follows from what has been said is that we ought to be careful about the sense in which we understand the term 'lay person' in Church usage. This term, as we know, is commonly used to refer to those in the Church who have not received the sacrament called 'holy orders'. We ought not to forget, how-

ever, that it is also used in secular life. There it means an amateur as distinct from a professional or an expert. Thus it might be said that I, who am a priest, have a lay person's knowledge of medicine or law. This would imply – rightly in my case – that I am an amateur in these fields, whereas a doctor or a lawyer is a professional or expert. From what I have said about the Church, it should be clear that the term 'lay person' may not be used in *this sense* to describe the position of baptised Christians in the Church. After all, the real 'professional' and the real 'expert' in the Church is, as I have pointed out, the true disciple of Jesus. To imply that only the office-bearers in the Church are such would, clearly, be very wrong. We ought not to forget, then, that when the term 'lay person' is used in Church language, it is being used in a very *precise* and *technical* sense which is different from its everyday secular meaning. To say that by far the vast majority of the people in the parish – indeed almost all the people in the parish – are 'lay people', obviously could not, and does not, mean that they are all amateur Christians and that the priest alone is a professional, expert one.

The Christian's relation to the parish
A fourth and final relevant point follows from what I have said about the nature of the Church. It concerns the way in which people ought to see themselves in relation to their parish. If we see the Church as a whole, and the parish in particular, as being basically people who are interested in following Jesus of Nazareth, then no baptised person may see the Church or the parish as something apart from himself or herself. Clearly people should see it rather as a family or a community of which they are members – fully and equally mem-

bers, as I shall point out in the next chapter. They may indeed be critical of the parish – and there may very well be many things about it of which they ought to be critical. But, in criticising it, they ought to remember that the parish is, and will be, as good or as bad as they themselves are – after all, the parish is *the people*. It might sound facile, or even glib, to people today to hear it said that the parish will be as good or as bad as they are. However, that statement is true, more true than is sometimes thought as I hope will become clear from what follows.

Chapter Three
Companions all

It sometimes comes as a surprise to people to hear it said, as I have said, that they are 'fully and equally' members of the parish and of the Church. The fact, however, is that they are.

Misplacing the Sacrament of Orders
One of the factors which often prevents people from understanding their position in the parish is a misconception which they have concerning the place and role of the sacrament of holy orders – 'ordination' – in the Church. In the past, at least, we Catholics placed great emphasis on this sacrament and on the sacred powers and dignity which we saw it as conferring. We were very conscious of the role and dignity of the ordained priest in the parish, and we spoke with a certain awe of the 'anointed hands of the priest'. In a sense, we saw holy orders as the sacrament which really gives status in the Church. This naturally resulted in a very clericalist notion of the Church. Even when we did see the Church more in terms of people than of institutions, we thought of it very much in terms of an inner group of people, namely, the teaching, 'ruling' group – the hierarchy and the clergy generally. In ordinary speech these were 'the Church'.

Today, thankfully, we have a better understanding of the place of this sacrament in the Church. Obviously we still regard it as a very important sacrament – one without which the Church could not survive. But we

20

are now aware in a new and exciting way of the important status in the Church which is conferred by three other sacraments – ones which every Catholic who is reading this book presumably has received. These are the sacraments of baptism, eucharist and confirmation. We now see that *these* are the sacraments which make a person a member of the Church – so much so, that anyone who has received them has become *fully and equally* a member of the Church. These are the basic sacraments. The sacrament of orders is secondary to them and is meant to be at their service.

In order to better understand the status in the Church which these three sacraments confer, I shall consider some points about each of them – points which the very rites by which they are conferred bring out. In doing this, I shall not follow the order in which they are celebrated today in the case of the initiation of young children – that is, baptism, 'first communion' (full participation in the eucharist) and confirmation. I shall follow the order in which they were originally celebrated, that is, baptism, followed first by confirmation and then by full participation in the eucharist. This, it might be noted, is also the order in which, according to the *Rite of Christian Initiation of Adults*, they are celebrated today in the case of adults. Celebrating these sacraments in this order has the advantage of highlighting the fact that the process of initiation into the Christian community reaches its sacramental climax when a person participates fully in the eucharist.

Baptism as entry into the Church
I think that it is true to say that even yet the idea which first comes to many people's minds when they think of baptism is 'original sin' and 'cleansing from original

sin'. Now it is true that baptism has to do with the remission of sins – something which would be obvious enough in the case of the baptism of an adult. It is also true that baptism has to do with 'original sin'. This is a concept which does not concern us here as we are dealing with status in the Church. All I need say about it is that, properly understood, it does express an important insight into our human condition, but it is not at all an easy concept to understand, nor is it one which Catholics always properly understand. However, interesting as the concept is, it would be a mistake to allow it to distract us here.

The point which I want to make is that if we think of baptism *first of all* in terms of the remission of sin, we run a very serious risk of misunderstanding this sacrament. We might end up seeing it as having to do simply with the salvation of the individual concerned and, therefore, as being a purely private, personal event. Indeed this is an understanding of baptism which is often encouraged by the apparently private manner in which it is sometimes celebrated. In fact, though it may come as a surprise to some to hear this, baptism is not a private event nor one which has to do solely with the personal salvation of the individual. Baptism is first of all a sacrament of *entry into the Christian community, the Church*. It is the first stage of a person's initiation into the Church, and this official entry into the Church is its first aim and effect. All the other baptismal effects, like the remission of sins and the personal sanctification of the individual, are, in their turn, effects of this first one. In this respect it is like being born. One of the effects of being born is that one can feel hungry. But its first effect, and the one from which all the others follow, is that it gives one life as a separate person in the world.

Somewhat similarly, baptism is a sacrament of remission of sin because it is first a sacrament of entry into the Church.

That baptism is first of all about becoming a member of the Church is brought out clearly in the liturgy of baptism. One of the most obvious pointers is the *minister* of this sacrament. Most Catholics know that anyone – parent, brother, sister, neighbour, friend – is capable of administering the sacrament of baptism, even outside an emergency situation. But they also know that the most appropriate person to administer it is a bishop or priest or deacon. This is simply because baptism, being a sacrament of entry into the Christian community, is bigger than a purely personal or even a family affair. As such, it should be administered by one who is commissioned to act in the name of the wider Christian community, and who normally does act in its name. Preferably it should be somebody who normally acts in the name of the particular community or parish involved. The appropriateness of the presence of such a person at the baptism points to something important about the meaning of the sacrament.

Another rather obvious pointer in the same direction is the *place* in which baptism is usually celebrated. We all know that baptism can be validly administered anywhere, even at home. But we also know that the most appropriate place in which it should take place is the community's normal place of assembly, usually the church – the building which in Irish we call *Teach an Phobail*, the house of the people. Even the place within the church where the ceremony begins is significant. It begins at the door – where people are normally welcomed into a home and a family. The minister spells out this significance when, at the door, he addresses the person by the newly chosen name and says, 'John (Mary or whatever), the *Christian community* welcomes you with great joy.'

Indeed the whole ceremonial surrounding baptism emphasises the same point. People sometimes think of the liturgy of baptism as consisting simply of pouring water and saying the words 'I baptise you ...'. In fact there is much more to it than this. A whole richness of ceremony surrounds the sacrament. There is, for example, the solemn signing of the person on the forehead with the Sign of the Cross, the public reading of the Word of God, the post-baptismal anointing of the head of the person with Chrism, the clothing with the white garment, entrusting the person with the lighted candle, the recitation at the altar of the Lord's Prayer. Through each of these ceremonies the person is symbolically initiated into the community and introduced to its treasures and its life – to the *Cross*, the great Christian symbol, to the *Word* which brings the community into being and by which it strives to live, to the cleansing, life-giving water of its *Spirit*, to the *Christ-like functions* for which it is anointed and set apart, to the *Newness of Life* which it is called to live, to the *Christ-light* which it is meant to be in the world, to the Christian *Family Table* around which it gathers with God as its Father. We in Ireland take baptisms for granted. Even yet, we sometimes 'celebrate' them almost 'behind closed doors'. We can imagine how impossible this would be in a situation where commitment to following Christ would not be taken so easily for granted. We can imagine what excitement there would be when the first step is taken in the initiation of a new member into the Christian community.

Confirmed in responsibility

In the early Church the sacraments of baptism and confirmation were seen as two moments in a single process of initiation into the Church. In fact, a person was confirmed immediately after being baptised – as is still done in Eastern Churches and in our own Church in the case of the initiation of adults. For that reason it is not easy to distinguish clearly and sharply between the significance and effects of these two sacraments.

Nonetheless confirmation does highlight a special aspect of membership of the Church. In this sacrament, more clearly and more explicitly than in baptism, a person is commissioned to take on *responsibility for the Church's task* and to become actively involved in pursuing it.

The solemnity of this commissioning is brought out by the *rites*. There is first of all the very ancient gesture, 'the imposition of hands'. This is a gesture similar to that by which, later on, both a bishop and a priest are commissioned for their respective special roles in the Church. It is an invocation of the Holy Spirit to assist people in fulfilling *public* tasks to which they are being commissioned. Its use in confirmation indicates that in becoming a member of the Church a person is called and commissioned to take on responsibility for the Church's task. Thus Vatican II says of people who are confirmed:

> Bound more intimately to the Church by the sacrament of confirmation, they are endowed by the Holy Spirit with special strength. Hence they are more strictly obliged to spread and defend the faith both by word and deed as true witnesses of Christ (*Lumen Gentium*, art 11).

Another pointer to the meaning of confirmation is the

use of the ancient rite of anointing with oil – which is now regarded as the essential rite of this sacrament. This has to do with 'christening' – a word which is very commonly used, but whose meaning is often forgotten. It means, of course, that a person becomes a Christ-figure in the world – it is a *Christ-ening*. Anointing is a suitable rite to express this. The word 'Christ', in both its Hebrew and Greek equivalents, means 'The Anointed One'. As a sign that we have taken on the Anointed One's name and the Anointed One's task in the world, *we* are anointed in confirmation – as we are in baptism – with the holy oil of Chrism. The very long tradition in the Church which connects *our* anointing and *the* Anointed One is referred to by Thomas A Marsh:

> The earliest references to the post-baptismal anointing associate it with the baptized person's assumption of the name of Christ: he or she is now a Christian … To be anointed in his name … means consecration to the service of Christ, belonging to him, taking his name, discipleship (*Gift of Community*, Michael Glazier Inc., Wilmington, Delaware, 1984, page 123).

In the light of this, it is understandable that there is great emphasis in this sacrament on the gifts of the Holy Spirit which are made available to us. But again, as far as this sacrament is concerned, we should see them as being made available to us, not simply for our own personal, private sanctification, but for carrying out the responsible task for which we have been commissioned. The precise public task for which we are consecrated and set apart by being members of the Church does not concern us at this point. What matters is that we see confirmation for what it is, namely a commissioning to take *responsibility* for the Church's task.

26

Partaking of the Lord's Supper

It is significant that, even in the case of infants, the ceremony of baptism ends around the altar. It points to the fact that membership of the Church means being part of a community which celebrates the eucharist, that full membership involves *full participation in the eucharist*, and that first communion marks the sacramental climax of one's insertion into this community. If we think about this we shall understand more about our status in the parish.

Reflection on the *family table* helps us to understand what our partaking of the eucharist says about our position in the Church. At home the family table is not just a place at which the individual members are fed. It is also a place around which the family gathers. It is a place where family members do not *just eat food together* but where they *share meals*. A point of which we need to be aware, especially if we are to understand the eucharist, is the difference between just eating food with others and sharing a meal with them. It is a difference which can easily be illustrated from everyday experience. When we are just eating food with others – as for example when we are eating with complete strangers in a restaurant or bar when we break a journey – it would not be considered outrageous behaviour if we were to take out a newspaper or a book and read it while waiting. To do this at a wedding reception or at a party or at the Christmas dinner would, however, be altogether unacceptable. The reason is obvious. In the cases just mentioned, we are not just eating food with others; we are sharing a meal with them. Sharing a meal is symbolic of sharing *life*. It is, for example, with a view to sharing our life with others that we occasionally invite them for a meal. When we are inviting them we do not at all think of ourselves as simply feeding them; our guests would hardly be flattered to find us thinking in those terms! To read one's newspaper or a book at a shared meal would be strange because it would be cutting oneself off from the others present and, so, would be contradicting the sharing of lives which is what the shared meal is all about.

Sharing a *family meal* is symbolic of sharing *family life*, with its common concerns, its commons joys, its common sorrows, its common struggle, the mutual support that is given, and so on. It is because of this that family members like to travel even long distances to come home for and be present at, for example, the Christmas dinner – here again it is not just to be fed that they come home. The family table in a home is, then, a focal point and a symbol of the family members' life together.

There is an element of *com-union* in every meal which is *shared* with others. And there can be *com-union* with the dead as with the living during such meals: at the Christmas meal the dead members of the family can be very close to people's minds. The word *companion* has something to tell us about the significance of sharing meals. A companion, as we know, is one who journeys with us on the way and with whom we can share our life. But the English word is derived from two Latin words, *cum* which means 'with' and *panis* which means 'bread'. A companion is one with whom we share life because he or she is one with whom we share bread – which is symbolic of our life.

The symbolism of shared meals should help us to see why partaking of the eucharist marks a stage further on the road to becoming a member of the Christian community. By partaking of the same food, we

28

enter into communion, not just with the Lord, but also with all the others who are gathered around his table – with all the other members of his family. Partaking of the common food at the common table symbolises, in a way that baptism does not so clearly do, the sharing in a common life, a common concern, a common struggle, the mutual support which membership of the Church involves. Partaking of the eucharist is communion with the Body of Christ in more senses than one. This, of course, is something which we will appreciate only if we see the eucharist in terms of *sharing a meal with others* in and through the Lord. A point on which we might reflect, especially when we are preparing children for 'first communion', is whether our emphasis is on eating food, albeit spiritual food, with others or sharing a meal, 'a sacred banquet', with others. The difference is considerable and important.

It should now be clearer why earlier I used the words 'fully and equally' members of the Church. When we share the same Christian food with others – with the ordained priest and with the rest of the people – we become, in every sense, their companions. In the parish the ordained priest and the other members of the Lord's family are companions. This ought to be a helpful thought – it ought to be helpful to think of us all, ordained priests and others, as companions in the Church. Companions will have different gifts and different tasks to perform. But they are equal: real companionship always presupposes the recognition of a basic equality.

Fully and equally members
Baptism, then, introduces us to the Christian community and to the riches of its Spirit-filled life; *confirmation* signifies that we have a responsible role in this com-

munity; when, in first communion, we participate fully in the *eucharist*, we give expression to the fact that we – all of us together – are 'companions' in the Church. We are, then, fully and equally members of the Church – as fully and equally as even the Pope is. After all, there cannot be a membership which is fuller than full. And, if we are taking words seriously, some cannot really be more equal than others. Remember that *every* adult Christian has been anointed twice over with the very same oil as that with which a bishop or an ordained priest is anointed in the sacrament of orders. This double anointing is really a token of the anointing of *the whole person* – something which was actually done in the early centuries of the Church. If we are conscious of the anointed hands of the ordained priest, we ought to be conscious too of the anointed head and forehead of every confirmed Christian – indeed, of the anointed person which every Christian is.

Different roles and functions

What I have said does not mean that there are not different roles in the Church, or that we do not learn in it, or that some members in it do not exercise the role of official leadership – a topic to which I shall return in a later chapter. I have already used the image of a family to describe the Church. In a family different people have different functions. The most influential learning of all goes on there and some members exercise what might be called an 'authority' or 'leadership' role – if everyone had the same role, the family would not survive as a unit. Still, in a family there are not, nor can there be, different degrees of membership. Once one is a member of a family one is fully and equally a member of it.

But the image of the family has its limitations too. This is because we almost inevitably associate the family with children, with the result that we might find ourselves thinking of our own position in the Church in terms of a child's position in a family. This would not be a correct understanding of our role. If we *are* adults – as anyone who is reading this book presumably is – then we ought not to think of ourselves as children in the Church, but only as *adults* in it. This, of course, is a standing in the Church which we must experience before we can become really convinced of its truth.

We might find St Paul's image of *the body* useful to correct any wrong impression which the image of family might give: in a human body there are many members, but no children.

Partners in a common task

To conclude this chapter, I return to the image of the family. Whatever a family is involved in, all the members are involved in it together – certainly all the adult members are. The concerns of a family – whether they be the well-being of a particular member, or the family business, or the mortgage, or whatever – are, or ought to be, the common concerns of all the adult members of it. The same is true of the parish. All who are full members of it are involved in it *together*, each with his or her different gifts and talents and opportunities. The mission of the Church in the world as a whole is the mission of the *whole* Church. The task of the Church in a particular area is the task of the *whole* Church in that area, not just of the clergy of the Church in the area. The task of the parish is the task of the *whole* parish. A Church or parish in which one group, for example the clergy, would be expected to carry all the responsibility, or would try to carry all the responsibility, would be as doomed as a family or a body would be in such circumstances. All who are equally members of the parish are *partners in a common task* and all have a shared responsibility for the common task. We shall see later that the spheres and the ways in which each member exercises responsibility will differ. But it is here, in *partnership*, that the future of the Church and the Church of the future surely lie. Karl Rahner, for example, clearly considered a sense of partnership in the Church to be of the greatest importance when he said:

> In practice, however, it would have most devastating results – and to some extent these do exist in fact – if the sum total of the individual Christian's conception of his own position as a Christian was that he was not a cleric and therefore had at most a subordinate and more or less passive part to play in the Church's life. In virtue of his baptism every Christian is one who has been anointed and consecrated, a temple of God, one who has been chosen and set apart ... Every Christian has a share in the active function of the Church both in her internal and external affairs (*Theological Investigations*, vol 8, DLT, London, 1971, page 72).

It is significant that the new Code of Canon Law is aware of the need for this partnership and that it suggests ways in which it might be structured and facilitated. At diocesan level, for example, it allows the bishop to summon a diocesan synod, that is, '... an assembly of selected priests and other members of Christ's faithful ... which, for the good of the whole diocesan community, assists the diocesan bishop ...' (canon 460). It allows him also to establish a more permanent advisory body called 'a pastoral council' (canon 511). This would be composed of '... clerics, members of institutes of consecrated life, and especially lay people' (canon 512, no 1). Its function would be '... to study and weigh those matters which concern the pastoral works in the diocese, and to propose practical conclusions concerning them' (canon 511). At parish level, it allows for the establishment of 'a pastoral council': 'In this council, which is presided over by the parish priest, Christ's faithful, together with those who by virtue of their office are engaged in pastoral care in the parish, give their help in fostering pastoral action' (canon 536, no 1). Of course, in this the law of the Church is being realistic: it acknowledges what experience of life generally shows; that is, that partnership, if it is to be effective, must be structured and facilitated. Relationships within a parish like any relationship – even the most intimate one – need to be 'worked at'.

Chapter Four
Servants all

An aspect of the task in which priests and people are partners which is often forgotten is that of *service*. I think that many Catholics, if asked what Church membership is about, would say 'personal salvation' or something to that effect. The emphasis would be on something which they receive rather than on something which they give. It would not, I think, be on *service* – at least not first of all. In saying that membership of the Church is about salvation, they are, indeed, right. But, if we think about it, we shall see that the matter is not so simple or perhaps so 'self-centred' as it might appear.

The Body of Christ

We shall see this if we recall that the Church is basically a community of people who wish to follow Jesus of Nazareth. This community, then, stands for, or ought to stand for, what Jesus stood for. To put this in another way, this community, the Church, is the *Body of Christ* in the world today.

The image of the Church as the *Body of Christ* is a scriptural one, found in the writings of St Paul. It is a very profound concept about which much has been said and written over the centuries. In 1943 Pope Pius XII wrote an encyclical, *Mystici Corporis*, exploring the rich truth about the Church which it tries to express. The image brings out the fact that, even on the super-

34

ficial level, the Church is a *body*: it is like a human body in that it is a community or society made up of many members with different functions to perform. But the image also refers to an intimate living union which, as Paul saw it, exists between the Church and its Head, the Risen Christ. It was for the purpose of emphasising this deeper unity that later writers began to refer to the Church, not just as 'the Body of Christ', which is Paul's term, but as 'the *Mystical* Body of Christ'. Here I shall concentrate only on the first aspect of the image – that of the Church as an *organic body* – as this is the aspect which will help us to understand the partnership which ought to exist between the members of the Church themselves.

The Church is the Body of Christ in the sense that it is that which makes visible his presence in the world today. During his life, Jesus was present to people through his physical body – it was that which drew people's attention to his presence, just as it is our bodies which draw attention to our presence. It was by *seeing* what he did and *hearing* what he said that people came to know and understand him in the first instance.

Today, of course, Jesus is no longer present in the world in that way – today nobody knows what his voice sounded like. But if he is to have any effect in today's world he has to be present in *some* bodily way – otherwise his presence would pass altogether unnoticed and would be ineffective. The visible way in which he is present to the world today is through the community of his followers, the Church. It is this which draws attention to his presence today, which speaks his word and continues his work. In that sense it is this which embodies him today – which is his 'body' in the world today. One of the functions, then, of the local Church is to embody Christ, to be his bodily presence, in the area in which it exists.

The Body of one who served

In the gospels, however, Jesus is presented, not at all as a self-seeking person, but as one who *served*. Thus St Luke's gospel says that he stood among the people of his time 'as one who serves' (22: 27). In St Mark's gospel he says of himself, 'For the Son of man did not come to be served, but to serve ...' (10: 45). Jesus was 'the man for others'.

Since Jesus stood in the world as 'one who serves', it follows that the Church, the community which centres around him and is meant to embody him, is, or ought to be – and ought to be seen to be – a serving community, one committed to performing a service. Furthermore – and this is what sometimes comes as a surprise to people – all who are members of this community are themselves called to be involved in performing this service – are themselves called to be of service. 'The disciple is not superior to his teacher ... It is enough for the disciple that he should grow to be like his teacher ...' (Mt 10:24-5). One cannot be said to be a serious member of a body whose function it is to serve unless one regards oneself as being jointly responsible for this service.

Once we see this, we can also see how inadequate an individualistic or self-centred view of the Church is. We can see, for example, how inadequate it is to think of the Church as, in Karl Rahner's phrase, 'a spiritual supermarket' in which each one does his or her own private, personal spiritual shopping, quite regardless of others around. The truth is that, in belonging to the Church, we are part of a service-orientated community *and* a community of people who are themselves committed to service – a community which is committed to performing a service in the area in which it exists.

It is within the framework of this understanding of the Church's function that we should see the connection between personal salvation and Church membership. Personal salvation – final personal fulfilment – is something which everyone naturally feels urged to seek. Hopefully it will follow – as God's gift – from living out Church membership. But since this latter means *service*, we can see that 'it is in giving that we receive'.

As I have said, people do not often think of it in this way. They often think that it is the sacrament of orders which calls a person to serve in the Church. They see baptism as simply entitling people to *receive* something from the Church and, consequently, they see the baptised as being simply at the receiving-end in the Church. It is true, indeed, that everyone in the Church – including the clergy – needs the Church with its 'companionship' in faith and hope and love, its scriptures and sacraments. To that extent everyone in the Church is at its receiving-end – as everyone in a family is at the receiving-end of the family. But it is equally true that *no one* is called simply to be served by the Church, but rather that *everyone* in it is called to serve in it – to be a partner in service.

Partnership in the Church's ministry
This means that everyone is called to be a partner in the Church's *ministry*. This too might come as a surprise to people. People often think that there is only one minister in the parish. But partnership in the Church's ministry follows from what has been said.

The word 'ministry' means 'service'. Since the Church's task is one of service, it is called a 'ministry'. All who are partners in this service are, therefore, partners in this ministry. Karl Rahner brings out the seriousness of this call:

> ...the Church as a whole, and therefore all her members – including, therefore the so-called laity – have been entrusted with a ministry ... This universal Christian *diakonia* (i.e. ministry), binding in the same way upon clergy and layfolk alike, is a Christian duty which no individual can transfer to the rest. In this universal *diakonia* (ministry) each has a responsibility towards all, and each Christian has a responsibility not only towards his fellow Christians but essentially towards every man as well (*Theological Investigations*, vol 12, DLT, London, 1974, page 71).

In fact, we often experience the parish as a community in which there is *one* minister, the priest. It should, however, be experienced as, in the phrase of Gerard Egan, a 'ministering community and a community of ministers' (*The Parish in Community and Ministry*, ed. E E Whitehead, Paulist Press, NY, 1978, page 73).

How precisely we are to understand the ministry to which membership of the Church calls us will become clear only after we have explored what exactly the ministry of the Church is. We shall discover, I believe, that this ministry is wider than is often thought. All that needs to be said at this stage is that it is not to be identified with the ministry of the clergy. To do that would be to say that the task of the Church is the task of the clergy – which, as I have pointed out, is not the case. As everyone knows, the clergy have their own special role in carrying out the Church's ministry – a role to which I shall return in a later chapter. They are given this role – they are 'ordained' to it – in the sacrament of orders. Baptism, eucharist and confirmation do not set people apart for the particular role which the clergy have in carrying out the Church's ministry. These sacraments do, however, call them to be *in their own way* involved in, and to take responsibility for the Church's ministry.

Chapter Five
The Servant of the Kingdom

Since the Church is the Body of Christ in the world today, there is only one way of finding out more about the service or ministry to which it is called, and that is by finding out what Jesus stood for and served in his own day. This is something about which every Christian has fairly definite ideas. They know that he stood for his Father's will, for salvation, for eternal life, and for true religion generally. And, of course, they are correct in this.

However, it is possible to have too narrow and too spiritual a concept of the ministry of Jesus. If we have, then we shall also have too narrow a concept of the ministry of the Church and, as a result, we shall never really understand the service to which baptism calls us or what it is that partnership in the parish is about.

In this chapter I want to show that the mission of Jesus was broader and more earthly than is often thought.

1. The background: wounded people

Each of the four gospels emphasises different aspects of Jesus and his mission. Still, there is much which is common to all four. In particular, all four set his ministry against the background of a wounded people. If we are to understand what Jesus stood for we must examine this background in some detail.

Wounded People

A person needs have no more than a superficial knowledge of the gospels to know the type of people with whom Jesus most associated. The list includes such people as the deaf and the dumb, the lame and the lepers, the blind, the 'possessed', the sick, tax-collectors, and sinners. These play such an important part in the ministry of Jesus that we cannot understand what he stood for without reference to them. As Albert Nolan says:

> It may be possible to understand Napoleon without understanding the history of suffering in his time but it is certainly not possible to understand Jesus except against this kind of background (*Jesus Before Christianity*, DLT, London, 1977, page 22).

For that reason, I shall now consider these people and what they had in common. I shall take two groups – the sick and the tax-collectors. At first sight, these might seem to have had very little in common. However, we shall see that, in fact, they had a lot in common. These and all the others I mentioned, were all wounded and hurt people, and they were wounded in more ways than might be immediately evident.

The *sick*, obviously, were wounded in that they were suffering from sickness or an infirmity of some kind – for example, blindness, deafness, lameness, leprosy. Among these I would include at least some of the 'possessed'. To go into the question of demonic possession here would take us too far afield and we should not allow it to distract us. However, it can be said with certainty that often those who are described in the gospels as 'possessed' were people who were suffering from, for example, epilepsy or some other physical or mental disorder. Illnesses like these could only be explained at that time, in that culture, in terms of 'possession by an evil spirit'.

There is one point about the sick to whom Jesus ministered which can easily escape us today, and if it does we shall never appreciate the full extent of their hurt or the full significance of Jesus' ministry to them. That point is that in Jesus' day very often there was a dimension to the suffering of the sick which people do not experience today. That dimension resulted from the religious understanding of sickness which was current at the time. In that society an unusual infirmity was seen as a punishment for sin – thus Jesus is asked in St John's gospel, 'Rabbi, who sinned, this man or his parents, for him to have been born blind?' (9:2). People suffering from such infirmities, then, were made carry, not just the burden of their sickness – a burden heavy enough in itself – but also a man-imposed burden, that of being made think that their infirmity was a punishment from God. In a society which was so consciously religious as theirs was, that was a very heavy burden – indeed almost an unsupportable one. In fact we know that at least one of the many religious sects which existed at the time, the Essenes, excluded the enfeebled from membership. This community regarded themselves as the final community of salvation and so, in excluding the infirm from membership, they were saying that these were not in God's favour. So, the deepest wound from which these sick ones were suffering was not their sickness, but the social and religious stigma which they had to bear.

Tax-collectors also were people with whom Jesus associated a lot. These were not sick, nor were they poor in the usual sense of the word. On the contrary they were very rich – Zacchaeus, for example, who was an important tax-collector in the city of Jericho was, apparently, very rich. At first sight tax-collectors would not appear to have been wounded in any way. Yet they were wounded ones, and had, in fact, a lot in common with the sick. They were wounded because they were *excluded* – they were pushed to the margins of religion and society. This was so for the following reasons. The taxes which they collected were for the Romans, who were the foreign power occupying Palestine at the time. Tax-collectors, therefore, were seen as agents of the foreign imperial government and collaborators with the enemy. As well as that, they tended to exact more money than they ought to have – an abuse to which the tax-collecting system at the time left itself open. As a profession, then, they had a very bad name. In the gospels they appear as being almost universally unpopular among their fellow citizens. The extent to which they were excluded is clear from the fact that in the gospels people usually mention them in the same breath as 'sinners' – the phrase 'tax-collectors and sinners' is a common one in the gospels. In fact, even though they were Jews, in one passage they are paired with gentiles, that is, those who were not considered as belonging to God's chosen people at all: '… treat him like a pagan or a tax-collector' (Mt 18:17). Tax-collectors were wounded people, because, though wealthy and strong, they were looked down on, despised.

A Gospel Story
There is a story in St Luke's gospel which, I think, represents this background of human hurt against which the ministry of Jesus is set in the gospels. This story also gives us an insight into his ministry and will serve as an introduction to our reflection on it:

43

One sabbath day he was teaching in one of the synagogues, and a woman was there who for eighteen years had been possessed by a spirit that left her enfeebled; she was bent double and quite unable to stand upright. When Jesus saw her he called her over and said, 'Woman, you are rid of your infirmity' and he laid his hands on her. And at once she straightened up, and she glorified God.

But the synagogue official was indignant because Jesus had healed on the sabbath, and he addressed the people present: 'There are six days,' he said, 'when work is to be done. Come and be healed on one of those days and not on the sabbath'. But the Lord answered him. 'Hypocrites!' he said, 'Is there one of you who does not untie his ox or his donkey from the manger on the sabbath and take it out for watering? And this woman, a daughter of Abraham whom Satan has held bound these eighteen years – was it not right to untie her bonds on the sabbath day?' When he said this, all his adversaries were covered with confusion, and all the people were overjoyed at all the wonders he worked (Lk 13:10-7).

The woman in this story can be taken as a symbol of the wounded ones to whom Jesus ministered. She was 'held bound', 'bent double', 'enfeebled', 'unable to stand upright', first of all physically in that she was suffering from an infirmity. But, there was much more to her suffering than that – as I said earlier, if we fail to see this we shall fail to appreciate the full significance of what Jesus did for her and, indeed, for many like her. Her deepest wound came from the low standing which she had in people's eyes. By the very fact that she was a woman she was, of course, disadvantaged in those days. It is true that, as Xavier Léon-Dufour says,

'The place which woman held among Jews was higher than that which was usually allotted her in the ancient world'. Still, as the same author points out '… the Law considers her as second in rank' (*Dictionary of Biblical Theology*, Chapman, London, 1967, pages 582-3). But her infirmity left her in an even worse position. In that society, religion had such an important place that, in order to have good standing, it was essential to be seen to be in God's favour. The woman, however, was given to believe that her physical condition was due to the presence in her of 'an evil spirit', and that, therefore, she was in the possession of Satan rather than God. She was, then, prevented from facing life and people as a dignified human being. She was 'held bound', not just by sickness, but by people, by a system – a religious one as it happened. The synagogue official represented that system: he was enslaved to it himself; he wanted to keep her enslaved to it, and also to enslave Jesus to it.

The phrases which are used in the story to describe the woman's condition, are, I think, good ones to describe the whole background of wounded and hurt humanity against which the ministry of Jesus is set in the gospels. They describe what all the different wounded ones, from the wealthy tax-collectors to the poor, from the blind to the 'possessed', had in common. Clearly what they had in common was not, as is sometimes thought, sickness or poverty. It was, rather, that each of them was 'held bound', 'left enfeebled', 'bent double', in such a way that they were 'unable to stand upright' in life.

Sin

The phrases also express something very profound about what *sin* is, and help to explain why sin was a major element in the background to the ministry of Jesus. People sometimes think that the reason sin is wrong is that it is the violation of a law imposed on us by God 'just to test our obedience' or 'to ensure that we behave in a particular way'. That is not the case. Sin is wrong because it is evil in itself, and not because someone, not even God, just decided to make it evil. We shall see this if we reflect briefly on what sin is.

Sin, all sin, is basically selfishness. Selfishness, of course, must not be confused with love of self. This latter is a virtue – after all, if *God* sees us as lovable, as we believe God does, then *we* ought to see ourselves as lovable and, therefore, ought to love ourselves. Selfishness is not love of self, but putting ourselves before others, using others simply for our own advantage, abusing others. It requires little enough reflection to see that it is really selfishness which underlies and characterises all our sins – our greed, our abuse of power, all our injustice, violence and so on. Since sin is selfishness, we can see that it is evil because of what it does to human living and human life.

In the first place, it distorts our *personal* existence. In abusing other things, we destroy the proper relationship which we ought to have with the world around us – that is, one based on reverence and respect. In abusing other people, we destroy the true relationship which we ought to have with our fellow human beings – that is, one based on equality and love. In abusing other things and other people, we also destroy the true relationship which we ought to have with the One who creates and loves them all. In this way, we destroy, if I might put it this way, the true relationship which we ought to have with ourselves. We fail to be, for God and for others and for ourselves, what we are capable of being and what we ought to be. Indeed, one of the main words used for sin in the Bible literally means 'missing the mark', 'failing to attain the goal'.

In the second place sin affects the existence of *the whole race*. It destroys the peace, the harmony, the order, the unity – the community – which ought to exist among people. It makes impossible that peaceful situation so imaginatively described in the Book of Genesis as one in which people 'felt no shame in front of each other', with God among them 'walking in the garden in the cool of the day' (2:25; 3:8).

The deepest truth about sin is that it diminishes us as people. In doing so, it, more than anything else, leaves us wounded, enfeebled, bent double, holds us bound, and prevents us from standing upright in life. It was a major element in the background of Jesus' ministry to a wounded humanity, because it is itself at the same time both humanity's deepest wound and the cause of humanity's deepest hurts.

II. Jesus against this background

Our story about the woman who was bent double helps us to see how Jesus stood out against this background of wounded and hurt people.

Involved
First of all, Jesus was very sensitive to, and deeply involved with this human hurt. We might notice how sensitive he was to the presence of the woman in the story. It was not she who approached him – perhaps she would not have dared, given her low standing among the people present. It was Jesus himself who took the initiative: 'When Jesus saw her he called her over … and he laid his hands on her'. Jesus was in-

volved with all the wounded ones – with, for example, 'sinners', the sick, and the tax-collectors. He invited himself to the house of Zacchaeus the wealthy tax-collector (Lk 19:1-10). Zacchaeus is only one example of the rejected ones with whom he associated. St Mark's gospel tells us: 'When Jesus was at dinner in his house, a number of tax-collectors and sinners were also sitting at the table with Jesus and his disciples; for there were many of them among his followers' (2:15). According to St Luke's gospel, he had a name for associating with these people: '... the Pharisees and the Scribes complained. "This man," they said, "welcomes sinners and eats with them"' (15:1-3). What is more, according to the same gospel, Jesus himself knew that he had a name for mixing with such people. Speaking about himself, he says there, '... and you say, "Look, a glutton and a drunkard, a friend of tax-collectors and sinners"' (7:34).

Compassion
His reason for associating with them was *compassion*. It was this which motivated his involvement with the woman in our story. 'Compassion' and 'pity' are words which are used frequently throughout the gospels to describe Jesus' attitude towards the wounded ones: 'So as he stepped ashore he saw a large crowd; and he took pity on them ...' (Mt 14:14); 'And when he saw the crowds he felt sorry for them because they were harassed and dejected, like sheep without a shepherd' (Mt 9:36); when he saw the bereaved widow at Nain, '... he felt sorry for her: "Do not cry," he said' (Lk 7:13). Compassion, Eamonn Bredin says, is *'the* characteristic of Jesus' message and ministry' (*Disturbing the Peace*, Columba Press, Dublin, 1985, page 117).

48

'Throughout the gospels,' Albert Nolan remarks, 'even when the word is not used, we can feel the movement of compassion' (*Jesus before Christianity*, page 27-8).

Critical
His compassion led him to be critical, harshly critical, of anyone or any system, even a religious one, which caused people to be wounded or which prolonged their hurt. Again our story is typical. The synagogue official invoked a religious principle, the sabbath rest, as justification for leaving the woman in her suffering, 'But the Lord answered him. "Hyprocrites!"' So, to say that Jesus had compassion for the wounded ones, is not at all the same as saying that he, or the Father whom he represented, was, in the words of Edward Schillebeeckx, 'a kindly granddad, disposed not to be very critical' (*Jesus,* Collins, London, 1979, page 143).

Healing
His compassion also expressed itself in healing. '"Woman,"' he said in St Luke's story, '"you are rid of your infirmity", and he laid his hands on her. And at once she straightened up, and she glorified God'. There are, however, two factors in particular which might prevent us from appreciating the full significance of the healing ministry of Jesus.
    One is the tendency to think that when Jesus healed, his motive was to 'prove' something about himself and his divine powers. This would be a very impersonal motive for healing anyone. As Albert Nolan says, 'His one and only motive for healing people was compassion' (*Jesus before Christianity*, page 36). Compassion, however, is not impersonal. Speaking of the *depth of feeling* which is conveyed by this word, Eamonn

49

Bredin says: 'The root meaning of compassion (*rahimin*) in the Bible is tender, vulnerable love. It speaks of … the tender response of those who feel for and with another, whose hearts go out, who are moved in the depth of their being' (*Disturbing the Peace*, page 117). In the synagogue, for example, Jesus did not call the woman over so as to make some theological point about who he was. He called her over because he was very sorry for her and wanted, as he said, 'to untie her bonds'.

The other factor is the tendency to see his healing ministry in purely physical terms – to allow ourselves to be so impressed by its physical aspect, which seems so spectacular as to miss one which is at least equally important. This other aspect comes to light when we think again of the way in which sickness and sin were so closely linked at the time. For example, in the case of the woman in the story, more bonds were untied than just physical ones. In noticing her, calling her over, laying his hands on her, healing her physical infirmity, Jesus also removed her shame and guilt. In relieving her of this burden, he enabled her to stand upright in a far deeper sense than physically – he restored her dignity. In doing this, he healed very deep wounds indeed.

Forgiveness
There was a similar factor involved in Jesus' ministry of *forgiveness*. In being an instrument of the forgiveness of their sins, Jesus freed them from the shame which was attached to sin in that society. He enabled them to stand upright, not just before God, but before others. Indeed, it is significant that Jesus is presented in the gospels as mediating forgiveness more by his deeds than by his words, more by healing people and assoc-

iating with them than by actually telling them they were forgiven – something which he is rarely presented as doing (see Edward Schillebeeckx, *Jesus*, page 206ff).

It is clear from what I have already said that healing people was itself a way of saying they were forgiven. So too was associating with them. Above all, the *meals* which Jesus seems to have shared so frequently with 'tax-collectors and sinners' were a clear statement of forgiveness. Sharing meals with people, I have pointed out, is more than just a matter of eating with them: it is an expression of intimate association with them, a way of saying that one is accepting them and bringing them into one's life – making them one's companions. When Jesus had meals with the wounded and hurt ones, he was saying that he, and therefore his Father, accepted them. He was healing their deepest wounds. As Edward Schillebeeckx says:

> Jesus' presence among the people ... offering or accepting invitations to eat and drink together ... with outcasts, publicans and sinners, turns out to be an invitation to enter in faith into a companionship with God: the intercourse of Jesus of Nazareth with his fellow-men is an offer of salvation-imparted-by-God ... (*Jesus*, page 179).

The ministry

This very brief account does not by any means tell us everything about the ministry of Jesus. But, as St John's gospel says, '... if all were written down, the world itself, I suppose, would not hold all the books that would have to be written' (21:25). However, it does serve to make the point which I set out to make – that the ministry of Jesus was broader and more down-to-earth than we sometimes think.

We tend to think of Jesus in terms of 'saving *souls*'. Jesus was, of course, interested in what is deepest in the human person. From what I have said, however, we can see that he is more fittingly described as being more interested in *people* than in 'souls'.

We can also have a narrow view of the salvation for which he stood. We can think of him as simply helping people 'to get to heaven'. Again, of course, it is true that Jesus was interested in the eternal value of every person. He was so conscious of this that in St Matthew's gospel he says, 'Why every hair on your head has been counted' (10:31). His desire was that people might 'have life and have it to the full' (Jn 10:10). The life which he offered was like a spring 'welling up to eternal life' (Jn 4:14). But we can see that he was also interested in the here-and-now and in offering people a better quality of life here and now. The salvation for which he stood was wholeness in its fullest sense – wholeness of body and mind and spirit. Untying *all* human bonds, enabling people to 'stand upright' in every sense, was what he was about. He stood for, and worked towards bringing about, a situation in which people can achieve this true wholeness. Since such a situation can exist only where there is love, he stood for *a deep conversion* – a change of heart in people from selfishness to love.

The servant of the Kingdom of God
A phrase which the gospels, and Jesus himself, frequently use to describe what he stood for and served, is 'the kingdom of God'. Jesus did not invent this phrase; it was part of his Jewish heritage. The concept can be easily misunderstood.

It might seem, for example, to suggest a territory.

We can see that Jesus was not interested in territorial conquest – this is what he meant when he said to Pilate, 'Mine is not a kingdom of this world ... not of this kind' (Jn 18:36-7). Since the phrase 'the kingdom of *heaven*' is sometimes used, it might seem to suggest that the kingdom has to do just with 'the next life'. We have seen that this is not the case – it has to do with people's happiness and wholeness now and not just after death. In fact, the word 'heaven' in the phrase refers to the place where God was said to dwell and is, therefore, just another word for God.

The kingdom of God refers to a *situation* rather than a territory. It is the situation in which God, not evil, reigns – scholars tell us that the phrases 'rule of God' or 'reign of God' are much more apt to describe the idea than 'kingdom of God'.

'Abba'

This brings us to consider one of the most obvious and distinctive characteristics of Jesus, namely his deep communion with 'the Father'. This was the inspiring force of his life. Thomas E Clarke describes the Jesus of the gospels as:

> '... the most creative and adult personality the world has ever seen, the man who has most decisively influenced human history, going about with the word 'Father' constantly on his lips, and looking continually to the Other as source of his very creativity' (*God, Jesus and Spirit*, ed. D Callahan, Chapman, London, 1969, page 97).

It would take us too far away from our present subject to discuss here why Jesus addressed God in male terms, or why he used the 'father' image more than the 'mother' image. After all, this latter too is found in the

Bible and was part of Jesus' heritage (see, for example, Is 49:15; 66:13). As Xavier Léon-Dufour says, 'There is in God such a plenitude of life that Israel gives Him the names of father and of mother' (*Dictionary of Biblical Theology*, page 328). We can take it that Jesus' choice of the 'father' image was determined largely by cultural and historical factors. However, the point which I wish to emphasise here is the intimate union which existed between Jesus and the One whom he called 'the Father'. This union was so close that, in referring to this One, Jesus used an extraordinarily intimate term, 'abba' – the term which a young, trusting child uses when talking to and about his or her father.

Being in such intimate communion with the Father, Jesus knew what kind of king the Father is. He is compassionate: '... Jesus speaks and acts in the name of a king who is compassionate, who does not make distinction ... He acts in the name of a father who loves all his children equally, without exception ... "who makes his rain fall and his sun shine on the just and the unjust"' (Eamonn Bredin, *Disturbing the Peace*, page 124). Jesus also was deeply in tune with, and sensitive to, the Father's vision for human life, to the type of situation which God wills for our world, to the form which God's reign or kingdom takes. We can see from the gospel accounts of his ministry how Jesus understood this. In his view, God reigns when people recognise the eternal value of their fellow human beings, when they show genuine love and care for them, and when they try to create a situation in which it is possible for them to develop their full God-given potential – in the words of St Luke's gospel, to grow 'in wisdom, in stature, and in favour with God and men' (2:52).

The kingdom or situation for which Jesus worked

and which he served is really one in which *human community* in its fullest reality exists. It is one of real companionship – companionship among people together and with God. It is that 'original' situation in which people 'felt no shame in front of each other,' with God walking among them 'in the cool of the day'. It is the situation which Vatican II speaks of when talking about the Church – one in which there exists 'intimate union with God and ... the unity of mankind' (*Lumen Gentium*, art 1). It is the situation which is very beautifully described in the Mass of Christ the Universal King as:

an *eternal* and *universal* kingdom,
a kingdom of *truth* and *life*,
a kingdom of *holiness* and *grace*,
a kingdom of *justice, love* and *peace*.

It is for the coming of such a kingdom that Jesus taught his disciples to pray and for which we do pray in the *Our Father*.

Chapter Six
Servants of the Kingdom

We are now in a position to see what, more precisely, is the service to which all the members of the Church are called.

At the mention of the ministry of the Church and ministry in the Church, people tend to think immediately in terms of *liturgy* and *liturgical* ministry. For example, the two new ministries most spoken of in recent years, and those most widely introduced in our parishes, are 'extraordinary ministers of the eucharist' and 'readers at Mass'.

It is a pity that people sometimes identify ministry in the Church with liturgical ministry. As long as they do that they will never really understand the service or ministry to which baptism calls them – that basic ministry to which *all*, both clergy and other members of the Church, are called.

Service of the reign of God

From our reflection on the ministry of Jesus, it should be clear that the Church's ministry is much broader than a purely liturgical one. Being the Body or bodiliness of Christ in the world, the Church's task is, as Christ's was, to be at the service of the reign of God in the world. Its ministry, therefore, extends far outside the church building and the liturgy into all areas of life – it extends to wherever people are struggling to be whole, in other words to wherever that kingdom of 'truth and life, holiness and grace, justice, love and peace' is not yet fully realised. It extends, therefore, to such obvious people as the sick and the dying, the bereaved, the young, the old. It extends also to married people and those preparing for marriage, single people, the poor, the unemployed, all who, in one sense or another, are trying 'to stand upright' in life – a category in which surely everyone is included.

Embodying the Gospel
The mission of the Church is often described as that of 'preaching the Gospel' or, since 'gospel' means 'good news', 'proclaiming the Good News of the kingdom'. Preaching the Gospel is, of course, basic to the Church's mission. But its mission is not simply a matter of *telling* people of the love and care which God has for them. It is also one of *showing forth* that love and care as Jesus did. The summary of Jesus' ministry in Galilee which is found in St Matthew's gospel, if understood in terms of today, is a model for parish life:

> He went round the whole of Galilee teaching in their synagogues, proclaiming the Good News of the Kingdom *and* curing all kinds of diseases and sickness among the people (4:23).

As Eamonn Bredin says:

> Jesus does not simply speak about love or compassion or forgiveness or good news. He translates this message into a way of life that is absolutely consistent with his preaching thus confronting his contemporaries inescapably with the implications of his message. We see the test of what he says in what he does. He engages in a whole range of activities which concretise the content and meaning of the reign of God. His preaching and his activity, his

message and his ministry are inseparable ... Through what he did people came to recognise the force of love that pulsed through life. In the company of Jesus, they became so aware of love's graciousness towards them that they learned to entrust themselves to it and to celebrate its presence constantly' (*Disturbing the Peace*, page 133).

A Church, say a parish, which would just preach God's loving care for people without witnessing to it in its life, could not be credible as the Body of Christ in an area. Its credibility would be at risk, not necessarily or primarily because of difficulties inherent in its doctrines, but rather because these doctrines would not be experienced as lifegiving – a point which a parish ought to bear in mind whenever it is faced with a falling-off in faith and in the practice of religion.

Here it should be helpful to refer to what Vatican II said about the Church as a whole being 'the universal sacrament of salvation' (*Lumen Gentium*, art 48). By that statement, the Council meant that the Church is called to be, not just an instrument in bringing about salvation, but also a sign of it – a 'sign of intimate union with God, and of the unity of all mankind' (*Lumen Gentium*, art 1). In other words, according to Vatican II, the Church as a whole is meant to be for the world *a sign of human community*. If this is true of the Church as a whole, it is true of the parish also: it too is meant to be, by its life of mutual love and concern, *a sign of community* – it is meant to be *seen* to be an embodiment of the companionship which it celebrates in the eucharist.

Servants of the Kingdom
It is only when we begin to see that the task of the

58

Church is to preach *and* to show forth in its life the loving care of God, that we shall begin to understand the service or ministry to which baptism calls us. For this task a parish needs much more than liturgy and many more services than liturgical ones. It requires a whole variety of gifts and talents and a whole community of people using their gifts together as partners in the service of the kingdom. For example, some in the parish will have a talent for helping the sick or the elderly 'to stand upright' despite, or perhaps because of, their infirmity. Others, perhaps young people themselves (the ministry of *like-to-like* can be particularly effective), will be gifted at helping to create for the young people of the parish a situation in which they can increase 'in wisdom, in stature, and in favour with God and men' (Lk 2:52). Others will welcome the opportunity of helping and supporting young people as they prepare to receive the sacraments of first communion and confirmation – of becoming, to use an exciting concept from the Inchicore parish, their 'faith friends'. Others still – again mostly married people themselves – will be good at helping married people to understand the special way in which God can reign for a married couple in their married life together: they will be able to open up to them the profound truth which Vatican II uttered when it said that their vocation is to be in their married life (as distinct even from their family life) 'a house church' – that is, an embodiment of that intimate unity and community of which the Church itself is meant to be an embodiment. Others, possibly unemployed themselves, will be sensitive to the needs of the unemployed and will be able to help them to experience what the kingdom of 'truth and life, holiness and grace, justice, love and peace' means in their difficult situation. Others still will be able to help the bereaved people to experience, even when faced with the mystery of death and loss and loneliness, something of that 'eternal and universal kingdom' – the people best fitted to do this might very well be people who themselves have had a particularly difficult struggle with the pain of bereavement. The baptismal call to ministry is a call to use one's gifts in ways like this in the service of the reign of God in the world. When people use their gifts in this way, the local Church will really be, and will be experienced as being, the Body of Christ in that part of the world today.

Public service
At this point I ought to refer to a possible misunderstanding regarding the service to which baptism calls a person. That is, the idea that it calls a person just to live 'quietly and submissively' the Christian life and, in that way, to be 'a quiet leaven in the world'. Obviously baptism does call a person to live the Christian life to the full. Indeed we should not forget that, according to the teaching of Vatican II, every Christian (and not just 'religious') is called to the fullness of Christian perfection – to be a saint. Without the attempt to live the Christian life, everything else a person might do in the Church would be a mere facade.

However, it would be a serious mistake to think that the Christian vocation is to be just 'a quiet leaven in the world'. Essential to the ministry to which baptism calls a person is the element of *proclaiming* the kingdom, of being a *sign* of it, of *witnessing* to it and, therefore, of *drawing attention* to it in some way. This was clearly an essential element of the ministry of Jesus – had there not been something very public about his ministry, he would not have been put to death on its account. Proclaiming the kingdom is, and always has been, an essential element in the Church's ministry. As Thomas F O'Meara says: 'If the first Christians had exercised only kindness and cheer, the Gospel would still be in the suburbs of Jerusalem' (*Theology of Ministry*, Paulist Press, New York, 1983, page 139). So, in calling a person to participate in the Church's ministry, baptism obviously calls the person to participate in this essential aspect of it also. In other words, it calls a person to *proclaim* and *publicise* the kingdom as well as to live its values. In that sense there is, then, something 'public' about the task to which membership of the Church calls a person.

This too can easily be misunderstood and, as a result, people can become discouraged. While all are called to be involved in proclaiming the kingdom, the precise way in which a particular person will do this will be determined by many factors. For example, as we shall see in a later chapter, some in the Church will be commissioned to proclaim the kingdom as 'official preachers of the Word'. But 'preaching', in the usual sense of that word, whether it be official or unofficial preaching, is not everybody's gift. Accordingly, not everybody is called to proclaim the kingdom in that way – not everybody is expected to stand up and 'preach'. Yet the fact is that *all* are called, not just to live the Christian life quietly, but to be involved in the Church's work in such a way that they will be recognised as being involved in it. Again to quote Thomas F O'Meara, and to put emphasis on one phrase in the passage:

… ministry has the *clear purpose* of serving the kingdom of God as brought and preached by Jesus. Ministry makes the kingdom explicit, turns its ambiguous presence into symbol, word, action (*Theology of Ministry*, page 137).

This, I believe, is an important consideration. The complaint is often made that people do not seem to see the need to be more than quietly present at the parish liturgy. This attitude would seem to be very understandable if people had no experience of being called to be publicly and responsibly involved in the wider ministry of the parish. There is, as we shall see, a very close connection between parish liturgy and parish life.

Gifts and talents

Since *gifts* and *talents* and their use, are essential to the vitality and effectiveness and well-being of a parish, some points ought to be made about this topic here.

The first is that, if they are to be used effectively, they need to be *recognised*. For the most part, we are not good at recognising our gifts. Even if we do sometimes suspect that we have a gift, we often think that it would be sinful pride to acknowledge it even to ourselves – not to mention to others. Here the help and encouragement of the community is essential – something which we might hope would be forthcoming in the Body of Christ. Indeed there are some people whose special gift is their ability to recognise the gifts of others and to encourage them to use them. The gift of drawing out the gifts of others is one which we ought to look for, especially in those who serve the community as its official leaders or co-ordinators – that is, in the case of the parish, the priest.

We sometimes hear about the need to 'control' gifts. This is a strange word to use regarding God's gifts, but presumably it means that they need to be channelled so as to be most effectively used for the *good* of the Body and of the kingdom which it serves. Today, they need most of all to be encouraged. As David N Power says:

Energy which is spent in stressing the need to discern and control spirits might be usefully expended in persuading the faithful that they do indeed possess the Holy Spirit and his gifts (*Gifts that Differ: Lay Ministries Established and Unestablished,* Pueblo Publishing Co., New York, 1980, page 134).

A second point which ought to be made about gifts and talents is that, when recognised, they need to be *developed.* We ought never, of course, to despise the natural God-given flair or talent. But neither ought we to despise the God-given ability to develop this talent. This is particularly true in an age of professionalism. If furthering the reign of God in the world is a worthy cause, then use ought to be made of every worthy means of furthering it. For example, those who are going to be of service to the youth of the parish, ideally ought to have given some thought to, and have received some help in, recognising and understanding the needs of young people and the best way of serving them. Those who are going to enrich people in their married life, naturally ought to have some knowledge of, for example, the phases through which a marriage often passes after the first romance fades: they ought to be able to help a couple, after this first phase has passed, to grow into an even deeper love for each other and, simultaneously, for God. They ought to be able to help them to find a new joy in their married life – a joy no one can take from them. Again, those who minister to the bereaved, ought to be aware of the possible stages of grief through which a bereaved person might pass, how to recognise a particular stage, and how best to help the person to grow 'in holiness and grace' even in grief.

Up to the present time we have been very conscious of the need to train people for the special ministry which we call 'priesthood', and, so, seminaries have been set up. Once we begin to see that others too are called to be involved in the Church's ministry in partnership with the priest, we ought to become more aware of the need to train others to serve the kingdom in *other* ways, whether this be on a part-time or full-time basis. This awareness seems to be very strong in parts of the Church. Thomas F O'Meara talks of some dioceses in the United States 'who do not see themselves as running primarily a Tridentine seminary but as developing a program of education for the full ministerial potential of the Christian ministry' (*Theology of Ministry*, page 10). One of the special needs and challenges of our time would seem to be in this area of investing in people more than in buildings.

The third point is that a person's gifts *will change* according to age and circumstances. One obvious example is the gift of *time*. This is a gift which is often over-looked, but its value needs to be rediscovered in an age of widespread unemployment. While unemployed, a person will, of course, be deprived in many ways. But the person will then have at least the gift of time more abundantly than while employed. This gift comes and goes in the lives of others too. The parents of a young family may have comparatively little time to be involved outside their home. They will serve the kingdom in the primary way in which a married couple is called by their sacrament to serve it: in their married life, they will strive to create a situation of 'holiness and grace, truth and life, justice, love and peace' for each other and for their children. In this way they will be *both* a sign and an instrument of the love and unity of which the Church is meant to be a sign and instrument – they will be the Church in miniature, 'a house church'. On the other hand, a couple whose children are grown up and perhaps have left the home, will have much more time available for additional service to the wider community.

Gifts will change too according to age. The gifts which a young person will have to bring to the community, will most likely be different from those of a retired person. What is important is that each one sees that baptism is a call to service of the kingdom of God, that each one understands what that kingdom means, and that each one uses in its service whatever gifts are given.

The parish liturgy

The liturgy of the parish can be understood only within the context of the wider service of the reign of God.

No one would claim that the Christian community is the only body in the world or in a particular locality which is interested in creating a better world. Others too have a vision for, and are working towards, bringing about a situation in which people can live life to the full. No matter where this better world, this better situation, exists, and no matter who brings it about, the Christian community understands it as being a partial realisation of the reign of God in the world. This, in the Christian view, is its deepest meaning and its deepest reality. 'The glory of God is people fully alive' – this is true no matter where such people exist. The Christian community might – or might not – be the only body in a particular locality which would understand and describe this God-willed situation as 'the kingdom of God'. But it has not a monopoly of insight into what would contribute towards bringing it about, nor is it the only body making a contribution towards bringing it about.

The Christian community has, however, its *own* special insight into it, its *own* special reason for being committed to its realisation. It has this because of what it is, namely, the community which is inspired by Jesus of Nazareth, now, as the Risen One, its Head. It would be impossible to say in a short space what precisely is the special insight and motivation which it derives from him, nor is it necessary to do so here. Surely, however, it has to do with the love, the crucified love, which must characterise this better world, with the change of heart which is necessary to bring it about, and with the conviction that a divine power which makes such love possible was manifested in Jesus and is released in the world.

The Christian community, if it is to hold on to its own special insight and motivation, must always keep closely in touch with Christ, the source of its inspiration. It must, then, have its own inner life of prayerful reflection and of intimate contact with Christ. In chapter two I explained briefly that one of the ways in which it imbibes the spirit of Christ is through the celebration of the liturgy. There, through signs and symbols, rites and gestures, it recalls, re-enacts, celebrates and enters into again, these events which are the source and inspiration of its own life.

Parish life and parish liturgy
But in the liturgy the Christian community does not

simply glory in the past and give thanks to God for Christ's life. It also draws inspiration and encouragement from it for its own present life of service of the kingdom. The liturgy of a parish ought, then, to focus on its own present work for the kingdom in the area – indeed also on its dream for the future of the kingdom in the area as well as on Jesus' work for it in the past. In other words, the parish liturgy ought to be related to, and in continuity with, the *life* of the parish, and ought to be experienced as such. It ought to be a celebration of the Christian community's efforts to further the reign of God in the area, as well as, of course, an acknowledgement of its constant failures in its commitment. Catholics are often reminded of the greatness of the liturgy, especially of the Mass. They are often reminded of the fact that, in the words of Vatican II, '... the liturgy is the summit toward which the activity of the Church is directed ...'(*Constitution on the Sacred Liturgy*, art 10). This 'summit' of Church life, however, must not be understood as being *simply* a celebration of the events of the life of Christ. Vatican II sees the liturgy as being also a celebration of the life of the Church:

> The liturgy is thus the outstanding means by which the faithful can express in their lives, and manifest to others, the mystery of Christ and the real nature of the Church (*ibid*, art 2).

If the liturgy of a parish is not experienced as manifesting the worshipping community's life of service, it will be experienced as an empty ritual. This will be true even though, from a technical point of view, it might be very splendidly and very beautifully celebrated, and even though, in particular circumstances, it might be very well attended. As the reader will have experienced – and as I shall develop at some length in a later chapter – there is death and resurrection involved in the life of service. It is this living for others which is, in Karl Rahner's phrase, 'the terrible and sublime liturgy, breathing death and sacrifice' (*Theological Investigations*, vol 14, page 169). This is the 'liturgy' from which the Cross of Jesus emerged and which alone gave it its meaning. It is the 'liturgy' which must be experienced if the parish Mass is to be experienced as other than empty – or, to use a word commonly used of it today, 'boring'.

Liturgical ministries
What I have said about the link between life and liturgy in general terms, is also true of liturgical *ministries*. If these are experienced as divorced from a broader service of the kingdom, it will be difficult to avoid getting an impression of falseness, even phoneyness. For example, it would surely seem strange if a 'eucharistic minister' were to be seen as one who shows care for the Body of Christ only in the eucharist and not for the Body of Christ in the community, or if the person who brings communion to the sick of the parish were one who otherwise shows little care for them. Something similar can be said of those who read or proclaim the Word of God at Mass – naturally it would seem false if, though *proclaiming* before the assembled people the Good News of God's love and care for them, they showed little interest in otherwise embodying that loving care.

The introduction of new liturgical ministries which we are experiencing today is good and important. While acknowledging the special ministry to which ordination sets a person apart, these new ministries emphasise in a new way the partnership which ought to exist between the priest and the people. Still, in the excitement of establishing new liturgical ministries, we ought not to forget old ones. After all, even before the renewal which resulted from Vatican II, people were contributing in important ways to the liturgical celebration of the kingdom. We can think immediately of the parish sacristan, the parish organist, the director of the parish choir. Important services such as these ought to be recognised for what they are, namely liturgical ministries on behalf of the kingdom of God.

Renewal of liturgy and renewal of life
However, an over-emphasis on liturgy and liturgical ministries might easily distract us. It might prevent us from seeing the need for renewal in other areas of parish life. Questions about liturgy are not the only ones or even the most fundamental ones which a parish should be asking. Likewise new liturgical ministries, good and important as they are, are not by any means the only ones which need to be encouraged in a parish. This is a point which David N Power makes. Speaking about situations in which liturgy is celebrated, but in which there is otherwise little evidence of the existence of *a community of love*, a situation in which 'the reality of Church life' is not evident, he says:

In such a context, questions about the liturgical ministry of the laity do not appear as the primary concerns of the local church. It is of more fundamental importance that lay people play a part in spreading the Gospel and in building up true communities of faith and Christian charity (*Gifts that Differ*, page 13).
What is of fundamental importance for a local Church is its *overall* ministry – that of proclaiming and embody-

ing in the area that kingdom which, to quote again the Mass of Christ the Universal King, is:

an eternal and universal kingdom,
a kingdom of truth and life,
a kingdom of holiness and grace,
a kingdom of justice, love and peace.

It is only when we see the task of a parish in this way and have this vision for the part of the world in which the parish exists, that the question of partnership and involvement in parish life ought to arise for us at all. When it does arise out of such a vision, we might be surprised to find that many of the difficulties which we usually associate with it, cease to exist. To quote David N Power again:

Lay ministries flourish in the context of a community of faith endowed with a sense of mutual service and mission. The question of lay ministries arises from such a milieu, rather than from a concern merely to increase the number of those willing to help presbyters and bishops in their task. Occasionally, it is in this latter way that the question is phrased, but it seems to miss the point. In short, in order to understand the reality of lay ministry we go first to the fact of community renewal ... (*Gifts that Differ*, page 133).

Each local Church ought often to reflect on its mission as described in the Mass of Christ the Universal King. It ought to ask itself in what areas of life the situation described there has yet to become a reality in its midst, and what gifts and talents are needed to make it a reality; it ought to ask itself, as Edward Schillebeeckx puts it: 'In ecclesial terms: what must happen here, within this pastoral unit, for the building up of a living community of men and women?' (*Ministry*, SCM, London, 1981, page 135). If it does reflect in this way, it will find that *many* gifts and talents, and *many* different people, working together in partnership, are necessary if Christ's Body is to accomplish its mission in that locality today. It will find too that the Spirit has made more of these gifts available than, perhaps, is sometimes appreciated. Bishop Michael Murphy of Cork and Ross sees the challenge which this presents to his own dioceses:

> There is a great challenge ahead. The challenge for each parish today is to utilise the talent of its members, to identify the needs of the community, and to harness the resources of the community to fulfil these needs. If we are to face the challenge that lies ahead, I feel it is necessary to set out again our vision for the future, and to outline the steps that need to be taken at diocesan and parish level, in order to achieve it (*The Parish — The Challenge Ahead*, page 7).

Chapter Seven
A parish in Corinth

Regarding everyday life in the first Churches, when the Christian community was fresh from the original experience of the life, death and resurrection of Jesus, the New Testament does not give us a detailed picture. For much of our information on the matter, we rely on letters like those of St Paul. Since these are *letters*, each of them was written to a particular 'parish' or local Church, or to a person who played an important part in forming the early Churches, and each deals with the particular problems and questions which the author thought needed to be dealt with in the situation. The letters, therefore, were not written with us in the twentieth century in mind and, so, do not give us a plan for organising parish life today. They do, however, capture for us something of the *atmosphere* and the *spirit* which pervaded these Churches and, in doing so, can inspire us in our vision for the parish today.

One passage which is particularly helpful in giving us the pulse of life in an early Church is found in one of the letters which St Paul wrote to the 'parish' in Corinth. I say 'parish', not because I want to distinguish it from a modern diocese, but rather to refer to a local Church. The young Christian community in Corinth was a relatively small group of people living in a large pagan city. Their experience of Church life must have been *very* different from ours almost twenty centuries later. However, it would have been closer to our experience of a parish than our experience of a diocese. For that reason, I speak of the Church in Corinth as a 'parish'.

The *details* of the problem with which Paul is dealing in the passage, which I quote below, do not concern us here. It is enough for our purposes to know what the overall problem was: it had to do with gifts which members of the parish had, or were claiming to have, and which apparently caused some rivalry in the community.

Throughout the passage Paul refers to different types of people like 'apostles', 'teachers', 'preachers', of various kinds, and so on. While reading the passage here, do not try to understand the precise role which each of these had in the Corinthian community – for example, do not presume that the word 'apostle' refers to one of the 'Twelve', or, of course, that by 'prophet' is meant one who foretells the future. Scholars tell us that even they do not always know the precise 'job specifications' of the various people referred to in the passage. It is enough for our present purposes to try to experience the *atmosphere* of the parish of Corinth without trying to get a detailed picture of life there. The following is the passage to which I am referring:

There is a variety of gifts but always the same Spirit; there are all sorts of service to be done, but always to the same Lord; working in all sorts of different ways in people, it is the same God who is working in all of them. The particular way in which the Spirit is given to each person is for a good purpose. One may have the gift of preaching with wisdom given him by the Spirit; another may have the gift of preaching instruction given him by the same Spirit; and another the gift of faith given by the same Spirit; another again the gift of healing, through this one Spirit; one, the power of miracles; another, prophecy; another the gift of recognising spirits; another the gift of tongues and another the ability to interpret them. All these are the work of one and the same Spirit, who distributes different gifts to different people just as he chooses.

Just as a human body, though it is made up of many parts, is a single unit because all these parts, though many, make one body, so it is with Christ. In the one Spirit we were all baptised, Jews as well as Greeks, slaves as well as citizens, and one Spirit was given to us all to drink.

Nor is the body to be identified with any one of its many parts. If the foot were to say, 'I am not a hand and so I do not belong to the body', would that mean that it stopped being part of the body? If the ear were to say, 'I am not an eye, and so I do not belong to the body' would that mean that it was not a part of the body? If your whole body was just one eye, how would you hear anything? If it was just one ear, how would you smell anything?

Instead of that, God put all the separate parts into the body on purpose. If all the parts were the same, how could it be a body? As it is, the parts are many but the body is one. The eye cannot say to the hand, 'I do not need you,' nor can the head say to the feet, 'I do not need you.'...

Now you together are Christ's body; but each of you is a different part of it. In the Church, God has given the first place to apostles, the second to prophets, the third to teachers; after them, miracles, and after them the gift of healing; helpers, good leaders, those with many languages. Are all of them apostles, or all of them prophets, or all of them teachers? Do they all have the gift of miracles, or all have the gift of healing? Do all speak strange languages, and all interpret them? (1 Cor 12:4-21; 27-30).

Like any extract from any letter, this one can be understood fully only in the light of the specific problems with which it deals and only when taken in its context in the letter as a whole. However, without going into details – and yet without having to do too much reading between the lines – certain features of life in the Corinthian community and some of Paul's thinking come through to us.

Partnership in the parish

One point which comes across is the great sense of involvement which existed in the parish of Corinth. Clearly it was not just a few priests who were involved in the life of the parish and who felt responsible for its well-being. Indeed it would be difficult to identify in this passage a person who exercised the role which we now know as the priest's. All sorts of people were active – apostles, prophets, teachers, good leaders, different kinds of preachers, helpers, people whose service had to do with miracles, people who had a healing ministry, people who served the community by recognising spirits, and so on. I might mention that we find that a similar situation existed in the communities in Rome and Ephesus. Thus Paul reminds the Christians in Rome that there are some whose gift is teaching, others who are preachers, others almsgivers, and others who do works of mercy (Rom 12:4-8; *cf* also Eph 4:11-2). It is clear that in neither of these letters does the author set out to give a complete list. So, if today people experience their local Church as a community in which one person, the ordained priest, is called and empowered to serve, while all others have a passive role, then their experience is very different from that of the early Christians in Corinth and indeed in Rome and Ephesus as well. As Thomas F O'Meara says of the New Testament Churches:

> The ministry of co-ordination and leadership was not the whole ministry, but one important ministry among others, with responsibilities and limits (*Theology of Ministry*, page 85).

The atmosphere in the parish of Corinth is very much that of 'a ministering community and a community of ministers'.

The body

The image of *the body* is a major one in this passage. The aspect of the theme which concerns us here is that of the partnership which ought to exist between the members of the Church. Concerning this, four points in particular are worth noting.

The first has to do with *diversity of functions*. Paul makes it clear that the well-being and effectiveness of the Church in a place like Corinth depends on *many* people performing *many* different functions in a co-ordinated way:

> There is a variety of gifts ... There are all sorts of service to be done ... If all the parts were the same, how could it be a body? (12:4-5; 19).

The second has to do with *mutual respect* – a point to which the official leaders in the Church might have to pay particular attention. Because the Church is a body, it would be wrong for any member to regard another member as unimportant:

> Nor is the body to be identified with any one of its

parts ... The eye cannot say to the hand, 'I do not need you', nor can the head say to the feet, 'I do not need you' (12:21).

The third has to do with *self-regard*. In the Church no member ought to be so dazzled by the obviously important functions which some members – for example, the ordained priests – have to perform, as to overlook or belittle his or her own contribution:

If your body was just one eye, how would you hear anything? If it was just one ear, how would you smell anything? (12:17).

The fourth has to do with the absurdity of *shirking responsibility* for the Church's task – of 'opting out':

If the foot were to say, 'I am not a hand and so I do not belong to the body,' would that mean that it stopped being part of the body? If the ear were to say, 'I am not an eye, and so I do not belong to the body,' would that mean that it was not a part of the body? (12:15-6).

The *unity* of a body, consisting in the variety of its organs, the *diversity* of their functions, and the mutual *co-operation* between the organs – that is Paul's model for life in the parish of Corinth and, indeed, in any parish.

Service rather than rank

Another point which the reader might notice about the passage from Paul's letter is the emphasis on *service* rather than *rank*, on *action* rather than *office*, on what people were *doing* in and for the community rather than who they *were* in it. When referring to the various people in the Corinthian community, Paul always uses *action* words – he refers to people by describing the service which they were rendering to it. This is clear in the case of such people as 'preachers', 'teachers', 'leaders'. But it is also true of 'apostles' and 'prophets' – the word 'apostle' literally means 'someone *sent* on a mission', and 'prophet' literally means 'one who *speaks* on someone's (God's) behalf'. As Edward Schillebeeckx says of the passage:

> Here concern ... was less with people and their status in the church than with what they actually do to create Christian communities ... (*The Church with a Human Face*, SCM Press, London, 1985, page 61).

This does not mean that the important functions which some members performed did not give them a special standing in the Church – Paul obviously regards some ministries as having pride of place when he says: 'In the Church God has given the first place to apostles, the second to prophets, the third to teachers ... ' (v 28). It is a question of emphasis: the Church in Corinth is seen as a serving community, and so, the emphasis is on *service* rather than rank. 'The early Christians described their service to the kingdom as actions and not as honorific offices ... There is no gulf between title and work, no substitute of personage for activity because the name of the ministry is the title of the minister ...' (Thomas F O'Meara, *Theology of Ministry*, page 88).

Words and worship

I referred earlier to our present tendency almost to identify ministry in the Church with liturgical ministry. You may have noticed the lack of reference to liturgy in our passage from the Corinthian letter. The reason, of course, is that the questions with which Paul is dealing in that particular passage are not, naturally, those about who might read at Mass or distribute Holy Communion – or, indeed, liturgical questions at all. The issues concern a much wider ministry which, obviously, was being exercised in Corinth. So, Paul is able to speak, for example, of a ministry of 'healing' and, in his letter to the Church in Rome, of services of 'almsgiving', 'works of mercy', 'administration', and so on (12:4-8). The ministry with which he is dealing is especially the ministry of the Word – most of the services mentioned refer to this. And even this was not an exclusively liturgical one – it included all sorts of activities like 'preaching', 'teaching', 'prophecy', 'tongues', and so on.

All this is not by any means the same as saying that the liturgy, particularly the celebration of the eucharist, was not central to Church life and to Christian identity in Corinth and elsewhere. Nor is it to say that eucharist and baptism are not major themes in Paul's writings. The eucharist was, in fact, being celebrated from the beginning – even before our four gospels were compiled. In fact our New Testament grew, to a large extent, out of the eucharistic celebrations and the memories and stories of Jesus which were recalled and retold during them. It is possible that the very passage with which we are now dealing was heard for the first time by most of the Christians in Corinth when, after arriving fresh from Paul's hand, it was read to them as they were assembled for one of their house-eucharists.

However, even though the eucharist was at the very centre of parish life, it was not by any means the whole of it. It was a focusing of their life of discipleship and a source from which they drew strength and inspiration for it. And since, in that sense, their life was not primarily a liturgical one, neither was service or ministry thought of primarily in terms of liturgy. What Nathan Mitchell says about the New Testament Churches generally might provide food for thought for a parish today:

In the New Testament, ministry does not organise itself around the liturgy but around building up the community's life (*Mission and Ministry*, Michael Glazier, Wilmington, Delaware, 1982, page 167).

Gifts and Spirit

I mentioned earlier the role which a person's God-given gifts have in Christian service. The reader may have noticed how frequently the words 'gift' and 'Spirit' recur in the passage from Paul – as, for example, in the opening verses:

There is a variety of *gifts* but always the same *Spirit* ... One may have the *gift* of preaching with wisdom given him by the *Spirit*; another may have the *gift* of preaching instruction given him by the same *Spirit*; and another the *gift* of faith given by the same *Spirit*; another again the *gift* of healing, through this one *Spirit*; ... another the *gift* of recognising spirits; another the *gift* of tongues ... All these are the work of the same *Spirit* who distributes different *gifts* just as he chooses (1 Cor 12:4ff).

Even allowing for the fact that Paul is dealing with a specific problem which had arisen in the Corinthian community, still his thinking comes through clearly: the way in which a Christian in Corinth was expected to serve the community was determined by the gifts which the Spirit had given; the right, indeed the obligation, to use these gifts for the good of the Church came, not from an appointment or an office, but from the fact that the person was a member of the Body.

The Spirit and his gifts today

Many of the gifts to which Paul refers seem unfamiliar

to us. In everyday parish life today, we do not find ourselves talking about, for example, people who have 'the gift of tongues' or others who have 'the gift of interpreting them' or people who have 'the power of miracles' or those 'with many languages'. Here I shall not attempt to explain the precise nature of these gifts since it is not our task to try to get a detailed picture of life in the Corinthian Church. Some points, however, ought to be made.

The problems of the Church in Corinth were very special ones. They were the problems of an infant Church, without long years of tradition behind it, trying to find its feet in a world which was often puzzled by it and in circumstances which were often puzzling to it. Clearly special gifts and resources were needed in this special situation. Clearly too the Spirit was with the Church, providing, in some very effective way, the gifts and resources which were needed.

That first century situation does not exist anymore. A typical parish today does not have *these* particular problems or need *these* particular gifts and resources. It does, however, have its own special problems. These have to do with finding a new identity in a secular world and as part of the global village. A point which we often forget is that the Spirit is as available and as present to a parish today as that same Spirit was to the parish in Corinth in Paul's day. Furthermore, we can take it that the Spirit is also providing today the gifts which the parish needs. To say otherwise would be to say that the Spirit has become less involved in the Church and less interested in it – has become in some way tired. This would be a very unchristian attitude to have. It would even be a subtle form of atheism.

The fact, however, that many of the gifts which are

needed in a parish today, are *new*, or at least *different* – different even from the ones which were needed fifty years ago – is an important consideration. Because they are new or different, and not those to which we had become accustomed, it is possible that they are not being discerned. Something of the Ascension story in the *Acts of the Apostles* might be happening again. There we find a picture of the apostles as if waiting for Jesus to be among them again in the way in which they were used to having him among them – a way in which he would never be with them again because it was part of a situation which had passed. If we can picture something like that happening in the past, we can picture it happening again. We can even picture it happening in a parish today. There too the concerned parishioners, people and priest, could be looking for Christ and his Spirit and the Spirit's gifts to be present among them in a way with which they were familiar – but one which really was suited to a situation which no longer exists. In that case, the question put to the apostles then would be relevant now: 'Why are you people from Annagh standing there looking up to the sky?' In that case too, the challenge to the disciples in the parish today would be similar to that which the apostles faced then: that is, to go back into their new situation and to find Christ and his Spirit and the Spirit's gifts in the *new* form in which they are present – a form which is suited to a new situation. Perhaps the gift which we most need today is that of being able to recognise the gifts which we really need today – gifts which, we can be sure, are present among us in abundance – and, having recognised them, to be able to foster and encourage them.

Chapter Eight
The priest in the partnership

That the priest has a special place in the parish is something which is surely obvious to everyone if only from experience of parish life. The precise nature of his role, however, is not always clear. It is, in fact, a topic about which there is much discussion among scholars today.

The priest as partner
One thing which is clear is that the priest is a *partner* and that he ought to be seen as such both by himself and others. The fact that he has a special position, even a particularly important one, does not at all imply that he is not a partner. We can see this if we think of the human body. There the heart and the head and lungs have particularly important functions to perform. Yet these organs, for all their importance, are useful only insofar as they work together with – 'in partnership with' – other organs.

I find that it does not come easy to people to see themselves as working in partnership with the priest. They seem to find it difficult to experience their involvement in parish life as being anything other than simply a matter of helping the priest to do *his* job. It should be clear at this stage that it would be wrong to see it in this way. It would be just another way of saying that the task of the *Church* is the task of the *priest* and that the priest alone is called to further the reign of God in that locality. It would mean that baptism, which is a call to follow Christ, is not a call to follow him in his service of the kingdom. Difficult though it may be for Catholics today to really experience this, the fact is that in a parish it is not a matter of the laity helping the priest to do his work. It is a matter of all the members working together, in partnership, in doing the community's work, the Church's work – their own work.

Lay apostles?
In this context the phrase 'lay apostolate' deserves comment. This has commonly been used to describe the involvement of the laity in the Church. There are, however, certain difficulties attached to the phrase. The word 'lay', as I have already mentioned, might suggest that there is something amateurish about the laity's contribution to the work of furthering the reign of God in the parish. In fact, their contribution can, of course, be professional. An obvious example is the parish organist's contribution to the Sunday Mass – this can be a very professional contribution. So too can the work among young people of a person trained in youth ministry, or that among married people of people who are skilled in marriage enrichment. Their contribution in their respective areas of parish life will usually differ from the priest's contribution in that area. But it need not by any means be less professional.

The word *apostolate* too can be misleading. Whether intended or not, it does suggest 'apostle'. This in turn suggests 'The Twelve', and these are associated in people's minds with the hierarchy of the Church. The phrase 'lay apostolate' might, then, seem to suggest that the role of the laity is simply to be *'lay* apostles' – 'amateur apostles', 'helpers of the hierarchy' or, in a phrase criticised by Leonard Doohan, 'an arm of the hierarchy' (*A Lay-Centred Church*, Winston Press, Minnesota, 1984, page 5). This could be yet another way of implying that the mission of the *Church* is the mission of the *hierarchy*, which would be like saying that the task of the human body is the task of the head. Everyone knows that the hierarchy have a key function to perform in enabling the Church to carry out its mission effectively and in a co-ordinated way. But it is a matter of the hierarchy helping to make the mission of the *Church* effective rather than the Church making *their* mission effective.

The role of the priest
When people think of the priest, they tend to think immediately of the sacred actions which he alone in the parish is empowered to perform. As a result, they often see his role as a mainly liturgical one. This, however, is not the case, as we shall see if we reflect on the matter even briefly.

At first sight, the sacred actions which the priest alone is empowered to perform seem numerous. In most of our parishes at the moment, he is the one who is the official preacher of the word of God, who baptises in normal circumstances, presides over the celebration of the eucharist, pronounces the words of absolution in the sacrament of reconciliation, administers the sacrament of the sick, acts as the official witness while two Christians are administering the sacrament of matrimony to each other, officiates at funerals, blesses in the name of the Church, and so on. When all is said, however, ordination to the priestly ministry is absolutely necessary only for very few of these activities – in fact, only for 'saying Mass', pronouncing the sacramental words of absolution and performing the sacramental anointing of the sick. That this is so is clear from, for example, the existence in the Church of deacons. The deacon, though ordained to the ministry of *deacon*, is not ordained to the *priestly* ministry, nor is he necessarily preparing for that ministry. Yet he is empowered to perform all the other activities which I have mentioned. Indeed in certain circumstances members of the laity can exercise many of these functions. The law of the Church says, for example, that 'where the needs of the Church require and ministers are not available' they can exercise the ministry of the word, preside over liturgical prayers, confer baptism, distribute Holy Communion (canon 230, n 3; *cf* 759, 766, 767). In certain circumstances too they can be delegated to assist at marriages (canon 1112, n 1). If there is a shortage of priests, they can be 'entrusted with a share in the exercise of the pastoral care of a parish' (canon 517, n 2) – something with which nowadays, in countries where there are 'priestless parishes', a suitably trained member of the laity is frequently entrusted even on a full-time basis.

There can be no doubt that 'saying Mass', and administering the sacraments of reconciliation and the anointing of the sick are essential to the priest's ministry – so much so, that a person who would not be able to perform these functions for the parish would not be able to minister as a priest there. However, the priest's role in the parish does not consist *merely* in performing these sacred actions. To say that it does would mean, among other things, that he is functioning as a priest only for a relatively short period each day – relatively speaking he spends at most only a short time each day performing these functions. But such a limited understanding of his priestly ministry would not really correspond to either his own or other people's experience of it. It would be to settle for the concept of 'a sacristy priest' which, I believe, very few would be willing to accept. Scholars tell us that on historical grounds too such a view of the priest's ministry is to be rejected. Karl Rahner, for example, says:

This narrowly ritualistic interpretation of the specifically priestly task is not only humanly intolerable, but also theologically wrong, since it is contrary to a modern ecclesiology and to the history of the priesthood (*Theological Investigations*, vol 19, page 80; *cf* Edward Schillebeeckx, *Ministry*, pages 139-40; *The Church with a Human Face*, pages 255-7; 265).

To understand the priest's role, and to see his role in the liturgy in context, we should reflect further on what I have already said about ministry in general. The involvement of the various members of the Church, using their different gifts for the good of the Body of Christ and its task in the world, ought, obviously, to take place in a co-ordinated way – otherwise there would be confusion. This means that there must be in the Church a ministry of co-ordination and leadership – there must be people whose service to the Body is that of co-ordinating the activities of its various members and exercising the role of overall leadership in the community. It also means that there must be some people in the Church, as in every community, who have *authority* to co-ordinate and lead; otherwise there would be a great risk of confusion. In other words there must be in the Church an *office* of co-ordination and leadership – there must be *officially appointed* leaders in the Church as a whole and also in the local Church. Since these have to lead a community which lives by the Word of God and celebrates the sacraments, they must be suitably equipped and prepared for such leadership; they must be empowered to exercise a leadership in regard to the preaching of the word and the celebration of the sacraments.

Experience of parish life alone would tell us that the priest is the one who, through his ordination, is so equipped and empowered. Scholars tell us that, in fact, it is in terms of this *pastoral leadership* – and not first of all in terms of liturgy – that the New Testament sees the office which we now call the priestly one. Speaking of the New Testament roots of this particular ministry, Edward Schillebeeckx, for example, says:

> Throughout the development of ministry in the New Testament one striking fact is that ministry did not develop from and around the eucharist or the liturgy, but from the apostolic building up of the community through preaching, admonition and leadership. No matter what different forms it takes, ministry is concerned with the leadership of the community ... (*The Church with a Human Face*, page 119; *cf* Karl Rahner, *Theological Investigations*, vol 14, page 208; Nathan Mitchell, *Mission and Ministry*, page 303).

We ourselves can see evidence of this in the case of St Paul. We know a lot about his ministry both from his letters and from the *Acts of the Apostles*. As we know it, his ministry is very aptly described as centring around 'the apostolic building up of the community through preaching, admonition and leadership'. We can take it for granted that in the course of his missionary journeys Paul celebrated the liturgy, especially the eucharist. However, it is not at all the liturgical aspect of his ministry which is emphasised in the New Testament accounts, but rather the broader ministry within which this was seen; Paul himself in fact never mentions that he presided at the eucharist, though Luke seems to do so (Acts 20:11; cf Nathan Mitchell, *Mission and Ministry*, page 168).

So, essential though the liturgical side of the priest's role is in the life of the parish, it is not the whole of his ministry. His wider ministry – that within which his liturgical ministry has its setting – is that of *overall official leader and co-ordinator* in the parish. Summing up 'the trend of all reflections on the subject today', Karl Rahner says:

> By analogy with the bishop, the priest is seen as leader of a Church, as leader of a community which really is the Church in that locality. He must, then, have all the powers which necessarily belong to such a leader of a Church ...' (*Theological Investigations*, vol 19, page 75).

The priest, then, is '... the proper and unique community leader sacramentally prepared for this ...' (ibid, page 78). Many facts of everyday Church life point to such a broad role. For example, it is to such an *overall* role, and not to a purely liturgical one, that the very word 'priest' refers: it comes from a Greek word, used frequently in the New Testament, meaning 'elder'. It is to such a role too that the word 'bishop' refers: it comes from a Greek word, also used frequently in the New Testament, meaning 'overseer' – the bishop's role of 'overseeing', as we know, is one with which the priest's is closely linked. Presumably too it is to such an *overall* role that people refer when they call the priest 'Father'. The role of official leader in the parish, however, is one which, as I shall point out later, can be easily misunderstood.

Leadership in the liturgy

This role as the official leader of the parish finds expression, for example, in the liturgy. We shall see this if we look at those liturgical functions which are reserved to the priest.

There is first of all his role in *the Mass*. That he exercises the role of overall leader of the parish here ought to be clear to anyone who observes him at the parish Mass. He stands at the head of the community – at the head of the parish eucharistic table. It is he who begins the Mass and gives the final blessing and dismissal. Throughout the Mass he prays, not in his own name, but in the name of the community – the word which he uses is 'we', not 'I': 'Father, *we* celebrate the memory of Christ, your Son' (Eucharistic Prayer I); '... *we* offer you, Father, this life-giving bread ...' (Eucharistic Prayer II); '... *we* offer you in thanksgiving this holy and living sacrifice' (Eucharistic Prayer III); 'Father, *we* now celebrate this memorial of our redemption' (Eucharistic Prayer IV).

This aspect of the priest's role as *presiding over* or *leading* the parish at the eucharistic celebration is referred to in the description of his role which is given in the Roman Missal:

Within the community of the faithful a presbyter (i.e. priest) also possesses the power of orders to offer the sacrifice in the person of Christ. He *presides* over the assembly and *leads* it in prayer, proclaims the message of salvation, *leads the people* in offering sacrifice through Christ in the Spirit to the Father, gives them the bread of eternal life, and shares it with them. (*The Roman Missal*, General Instruction, n 60 – italics mine).

The priest exercises the role of official leader of the

90

community in the *sacrament of reconciliation* also. This is a point which people often fail to see – with, I believe, serious results.

To appreciate this aspect of the priest's role in this sacrament, we must understand something which might easily escape us regarding the sin of a member of the Church. That is, that such a sin is always a sin, not just against God, but also against the person's brothers and sisters in the Christian community. That this is so becomes clear when we consider again the Church as the Body of Christ. Being Christ's Body in the world, the Church is called to be for the world an embodiment of his saving love. It is meant to be a sign which draws people's attention to this love and, in this way, to be instrumental in spreading it – to be, as Vatican II says, a sacrament of salvation. To the extent, however, that we its members are sinners, we are people who fail in love – selfishness, I have said, is the basis of all sins. Because of the sins of its members, then, the Church is less an embodiment of Christ's love than it ought to be, less a sign and reminder of it to the world and less an instrument in bringing it into the world. By sinning, therefore, the member of the Church prevents the community, brothers and sisters in Christ, from being what it is called to be for the world. It is for this reason that Karl Rahner could say, when speaking especially about members of the Church, 'No one lives for himself alone. And so no one sins for himself alone' (*Theological Investigations*, vol 2, page 139).

The Church member who sins needs, then, to acknowledge this sin not just before God, but also before the community, and needs to be reconciled not just directly with God, but also with the community. Indeed

91

it is significant that when we come together to celebrate the eucharist, the very first thing we do is to seek this reconciliation: we confess our sins, not only to God but also 'to you my brothers and sisters'. And we do something similar before we receive communion: before we approach the family table we offer one another the sign of peace.

Here I do not have to discuss how precisely the sacrament of reconciliation relates to these and other ways of becoming reconciled with the community and with God. It is sufficient for our purposes to say that such reconciliation can take place in a uniquely solemn, formal and effective way in this sacrament. Many factors contribute towards making it a special means of reconciliation. The one which concerns us here is the fact that it takes place in the presence of, and through, the priest. Here again there is a community dimension to his role: he acts as the official leader of the community who is empowered, in a way that nobody else is, to utter in its name the word of forgiveness and reconciliation entrusted to it by Christ. The priest alludes to this aspect of his role when he prays that in this sacrament God will give the person pardon and peace 'through the ministry of the Church'. If we do not see this aspect of the priest's role in the sacrament of reconciliation, we shall fail to understand many things. For example, we shall never even begin to see why this sacrament exists at all – we shall not be able to answer the question: 'Why confess to a priest? Why not deal directly with God?' Nor shall we appreciate the value of the present tendency to celebrate this sacrament with a 'Penitential Service' which attempts to involve not just the person alone, but the community.

The priest exercises the same role of official leader of

the community when he administers the *sacrament of the sick*. Here again people tend to think of him as simply representing Christ. He does represent Christ. But he does so because of his role in the *Body of Christ* – the Church. He comes to the sick person in the name of that community whose function it is to embody in the world Christ's love and care for the sick, and his power to triumph over sickness and suffering and death. Through the priest, the Church – and therefore, Christ – addresses to the sick person the sure promise of support in the crisis which serious illness or declining years can bring, the sure promise that in this crisis too the sick person can find that 'truth and life', that 'holiness and grace', that 'love and peace' which characterises the kingdom of God. This role of the priest as official spokesperson for the Church is referred to by Vatican II:

> By the sacred anointing of the sick and the prayer of her priests, *the whole Church* commends those who are ill to the suffering and glorified Lord ... (*Lumen Gentium*, art 11 – italics mine).

Since in this sacrament too the priest acts in the name of the Church, he should try to be surrounded, while administering it, by as many as possible of those whom, as official leader of the Christian community, he represents and whose care and support he is supposed to be embodying.

The priest as community leader
As I have already said, the role of the priest as overall, official leader in the parish can easily be misunderstood.

It hardly needs to be said that it would be grossly misunderstood if it were seen in terms of *power*: '...

You know that among the pagans their so-called rulers lord it over them, and their great men make their authority felt. This is not to happen among you ...' (Mk 10:42-4). Leadership in the parish is leadership '... in a community of brothers and sisters in which the power structures which prevail in the world are gradually broken down' (Edward Schillebeeckx, *Ministry*, page 135). It is not to be understood, then, in the way in which leadership or authority are commonly understood.

Obviously it would be seriously misunderstood too if it were taken to mean that the priest is the *only* leader in the parish and so has a monopoly of leadership roles there – a misunderstanding which would underlie, for example, the notion that the priest himself must initiate everything, not to mention *do* everything. We may not forget that the Spirit who was at work in the parish in Corinth is at work in this parish too. Therefore there will be people there who are gifted in ways in which the priest is not – '... working in all sorts of different ways in different people, it is the same God who is working in all of them' (1 Cor 12:6). They will be gifted, for example, in the Christian formation of youth, in marriage enrichment, in ministering to the sick, the dying, the bereaved, the unemployed, the poor, in university and hospital ministry, in contributing towards the celebration of a living liturgy, in adult religious education, in explaining the faith to the very young (a gift and a Christian ministry which we could all too easily take for granted), in parish administration, and in many other ways. Because they are gifted in areas and in ways in which the priest is not, these will be able to take initiatives which he would never be able to take – in other words in certain areas of parish life they will be able to exercise a real *leadership role* which he would be incapable of exercising. So, to say that the priest is the overall and official leader in the parish, clearly is not to imply that this other leadership potential ceases to exist; that would be the same as saying that the priest has a monopoly of the Spirit's gifts to the parish. Clearly too it does not mean that the priest, even if he wished to, would be entitled to stifle such gifts and initiatives – that surely would be a great sin against Christ and his members and the kingdom which they are meant to bring about in the locality. After all, all the other members of the parish are members of Christ's Body just as much as the priest is; they too are 'fully and equally' members of the parish. Therefore, they, no less than he, are called, and obliged, to use their gifts for the good of the Body.

The priest's role as the overall and official leader in the parish is quite the opposite to all this. As overall leader his task is *to inspire* and *to co-ordinate* – to inspire people with a vision for the parish, to encourage, as Paul did, the use of every gift and talent which will help to translate this vision into reality, and to maintain the activities of the other members in unity: 'he has the function of guiding and maintaining in unity all other functions and their holders' (Karl Rahner, *Theological Investigations*, vol 19, page 75). His particular service to the parish endeavour might be described in terms of a threefold activity: that of *drawing out, drawing upon*, and *drawing together* the gifts and talents and leadership qualities which are in the parish. Or, to use three words which the Law of the Church uses of his ministry, it is one of *recognising, promoting*, and *fostering* such gifts (*cf* canon 529, n 2). The 'collecting' or gathering together of the people's prayers which he does in the *Collect* of the Mass might indeed be seen as an expression of his wider function as a 'gatherer' in the parish.

When all is said, the priest's ministry is very much a *ministry of the Word*. It was the Word which called the parish into being in the first place – the parish is made up of people who are inspired by what they have heard and know about Jesus of Nazareth. It is the Word which continues to call it to be what it is meant to be and to do what it is meant to do. Therefore, the ministry of leading and inspiring and calling the parish is above all a ministry of the Word.

Bishop Michael Murphy, of Cork and Ross, speaks of the challenge which faces the priest today as leader in the parish:

A new style of leadership will be expected of the priest. This will be a participatory style, which involves: inviting people, promoting group discussion, listening, clarifying issues, identifying a lack of information, reminding the group of its agreed mandate. A sincerity of purpose, a respect for each person, and an openness to new learning are personal qualities essential to this style of leadership. ... It will be essential for him to develop some insights and skills necessary for promoting a participatory style of leadership. ... It can be painful and troublesome in the adjustment of leadership styles, but it can equally be satisfying and rewarding. The long-term benefits for the Church will be enormous (*The Parish – The Challenge Ahead*, pages 13-4).

Chapter Nine
Celebrating companionship

The parish Mass is of central importance in the life of the local Church. The Mass, as every Catholic knows, has a great depth of meaning – in itself it contains 'the Mystery of our Faith'. Of particular interest to us here is the fact that the parish Mass is an expression and a celebration of what the parish is.

The celebration of group identity
Before talking about the Mass, I should make two points about groups in general. The first is that every group needs occasionally to express and celebrate its identity – what it is, and what makes it be what it is. If a group were never to do this, it would soon lose all sense of its identity, it would even cease to be a distinct group. The second is that when a group does express and celebrate its identity, it becomes more conscious of what it is and, in a real sense, becomes more fully what it wants to be.

Some examples will help to explain this. One is our identity as a particular 'people'. To say that the Irish people have a common identity is to say that the people who live in places as far apart as Kerry and Derry, Cork and Cavan, Donegal and Dublin, are not just people who happen to live in the same island, but are in a deeper sense a distinct group, have a deeper 'national' identity and are, in a deeper sense, one.

For the most part, however, these people are involved with their different concerns in the very different circumstances and places in which they live. If their common identity never finds expression, it will die. If, for example, the people who live in Ballyhaunis and Ballina, and Cooloughra and Coolarne, never think about or express what they have in common with one another and also with the people in Wexford and Waterford and Wicklow, they will, sooner or later, forget what they have in common and lose all sense of their common identity.

The fact is, of course, that they do express and celebrate this. They do it, for example, on St Patrick's Day. On that day they *together* take a holiday and *together* express their identity, not just as a religious grouping, but a national one. This celebration of national identity actually deepens and strengthens it. After St Patrick's Day, all who are involved in the celebrations, or have been touched by them, are more conscious of being Irish people. Something similar takes place on, for example, All-Ireland Final Day. Anyone who is involved in that, either in Croke Park or at home through the television or radio, is caught up in the experience of being part of a wider group – a nation. The same happens in other countries. The people of Britain have, for example, Remembrance Day, as well as, of course, Cup Final Day. The people of the United States of America have Independence Day and Thanksgiving Day – two days which, celebrated together by everyone across a huge continent, help to sustain the common national identity which such diverse people share.

Remembering
If we think about the matter, we shall notice that an important feature of such celebrations of identity is

remembering, recalling, retelling the story. This element is obvious and is even explicitly referred to in Britain's Remembrance Day. It is not very far beneath the surface in the American Independence Day and Thanksgiving Day, both of which have to do with recalling and remembering events which made the people the nation which they are. It is also present in our own St Patrick's Day celebrations. Remembering our origins as the religion-shaped nation we are, is a big element in our celebrations. Though we may not be conscious of this, the fact is that the music which we play on that day, the songs which we sing, the poems which we recite, the plays which we perform, even the parades in which we participate, have a strong element of remembering, of telling, in different ways, the stories of our past. These are the stories which have made us what we are. Telling them again certainly reminds us of what we are and what we ought to be. But it does more: it helps us to become more fully what we ought to be.

The parish expresses its identity
The local Church too needs to express and celebrate its identity. After all, it too is made up of different people, working at different jobs, and of different families, with different pre-occupations and concerns, living in different circumstances in different districts. If all these different people do not occasionally express their common identity as the Church in this area, they will very soon lose all sense of being *together* the Church in the area.

There are many ways in which a parish can express its identity as Church, for example, through common projects on behalf of the kingdom. The most solemn and the most explicit way is, or is meant to be, the parish Mass. There the local Church, in its unity and diversity, assembles very formally *as* the Church in this area. As might be expected, the element of remembering is a very strong one in this celebration.

Recalling the story

This element is obviously present in the Liturgy of the Word. Here parts of the story which shaped the Church as a whole, and this local Church in particular, and which explain its identity and its purpose, are read. The reading from the Old Testament, if well chosen, can remind the community of its very ancient roots in the religion of Israel, the religion out of which Jesus was brought forth, and which so profoundly influenced him and, through him, the assembled community. The second reading is usually taken from the letters written to early Churches, or from the *Acts of the Apostles*, and it recalls moments or situations in those precious formative youthful years of the Church's existence. The gospel reading, the climax of this part of the celebration, recalls some part of the story of Jesus himself, as the early Church lovingly remembered him and faithfully understood him. The point of the homily is to relate those stories to the present life of the parish, to strengthen its sense of identity as the Body of Christ and its commitment to its task as his Body in that locality.

Re-enacting the story

The element of remembering is continued in the Liturgy of the Eucharist. Here the parish *re-enacts* something in remembrance of its founder, *does* something in memory of him. What it does in memory of him here is that very thing which, above all else, he wanted to be remembered by, that which, above all else, he wanted his followers to do in his memory. What this is, obviously has something important to tell us about who he was and what his Body ought to be.

It sometimes upsets people to hear the Mass spoken of as a meal. It would be understandable if it was being spoken of as 'just another meal' – though the profound significance of any shared meal ought not to be missed. The Mass *is*, of course, a meal – after all, it is a re-enactment of the Last *Supper*, in other words of the last *meal* which Jesus shared with his disciples. So, what Jesus wanted to be remembered above all else as doing, was sharing his final supper. What, above all else, he wanted his Body to do in his memory was to celebrate this final supper in its full significance.

Body given, blood poured
Already in chapter three, I emphasised the deep significance of the shared meal. I contrasted shared meals with just 'eating together' as complete strangers might do in silence or while reading newspapers at the same table or counter in a restaurant. *Shared meals*, I pointed out, shared bread or 'panis', symbolises shared *lives* – 'companionship'. What Jesus told his disciples to do in his memory, is not simply to eat bread as individuals from the same table, but to celebrate a *shared meal*.

The mind of Jesus at the Last Supper is brought out very clearly by the words which, at the very heart of our celebration, we recall him as using. People often miss the significance of these words. Often the words which they remember from the core of the Mass are the 'This is my body' and 'This is my blood'. This, however, is not an accurate account of the words attributed to Jesus in this part of the Mass. What we recall him as saying is:

...this is my body which will be *given up for you and for all...*, ...this is the cup of my blood ... It will be *shed for you and for all* ...

What we recall Jesus as saying might be summarised as:

This is myself – *given, poured out* – for you and for all your needs, even for the forgiveness of your sins. This is myself, *given* for the sake of your wholeness, *sacrificed* so that you may be able to stand upright.

What Jesus wants his gathered Church to do in his memory is not just to celebrate the Last Supper in a rit-ualistic way – that would be easy. What he wants it to do in his memory is to celebrate that last meal as the one which symbolically expressed, and summed up, and brought to a conclusion, his own life of self-giving, sacrificial service of the kingdom. What he wants it to do is to celebrate that meal as *also* symbolically ex-pressing and celebrating its own present life of service of the kingdom, lived 'through him, with him and in him'. What he wants the people of a parish gathered together at Mass to be doing is saying, or always striv-ing to be able to say – because this is not an easy thing to say:

Here we are, with you – given, poured out – for all, especially for all around us, and for all their needs.

The identity of the parish

The fact is, then, that when the parish gathers to ex-press in this formal and solemn way what it is, it *does* celebrate a meal – that last meal which Jesus shared with his disciples. Our problem often is that we do not find it easy to grasp the full significance of that last meal and what it says about who Jesus was and what the parish is. The meal which is celebrated is, or is

102

meant to be, an expression and a celebration of companionship in the service of the kingdom and of the concern and the self-giving which that involves. It is also meant to be a celebration of the power of Christ's own self-giving – 'unto death' – which makes such service possible. When we see the Mass in this way, we can hardly think of it as beginning in any other way than with a humble 'I confess', or ending with anything other than an exhortation to 'Go, in peace, to *love* and *serve* ...'.

Chapter Ten
Easter people

The parish celebrates its identity in the most solemn and dramatic way of all during Holy Week, the great week in its liturgical life. It does this particularly in the liturgies of Holy Thursday, Good Friday and the Easter Vigil. Like liturgies generally, these great ones do not just celebrate something of the past, something in the life of Jesus: they also celebrate something in the present life of his Body. They draw attention, therefore, to certain features which are, or ought to be, characteristic of the life of the parish.

The order which the parish follows in celebrating these events is, of course, the natural one – it begins with Thursday, goes on to Friday and then to the vigil of Saturday night and Sunday morning. However, so as to bring out the significance of the events, it is helpful sometimes to consider them in the reverse order and to start at the end or, rather, at the new beginning – the Easter Vigil. After all, this is the climax of it all. Without Easter, the rest would have no meaning and, so, there would be no celebration at all. Without Easter, Good Friday would literally have been a dead, silent end.

Easter

Resurrection – new life
Easter is first of all about the resurrection of Jesus. At Easter the parish celebrates the New and Eternal Life

into which his life of service flowed and with which it was finally crowned. It celebrates the final, victorious, joyful outcome of his life of service.

New life and the joy which it brings are features of every life of service. There is that paradoxical experience that in giving we do receive, that in losing our life for the sake of others we do somehow find it – that, for example, the time which we give to others, the thoughts of which we let go when we listen to others, though lost, are somehow replaced by something new and better.

In its service of the kingdom, the parish will have had its own resurrection experiences. It will have had glimpses of the slow emergence of new life both within itself and around it. It will have noticed little ways, and even great ways, in which selfishness can give way to love, in which sin can be overcome by God's grace, in which the darkness in human life can be slowly dispelled, in which situations which are potentially destructive of human living can be transformed into life-giving ones. It would indeed be a pity if, during the Easter Vigil, the parish failed to reflect on this aspect of its own life of service and to see that even already it has experienced something of the new life and joy of Easter. It would be a pity if it did not celebrate, and rejoice in, and give thanks for this too.

Of course, the parish has not yet experienced the final coming of the kingdom. As it celebrates Easter, it knows that there still exist, both within itself and in the world around it, many dark, destructive, death-bearing forces. Perhaps it is conscious of this in a new way in a nuclear age. The presence of these forces can often be a threat to its hope – even as it celebrates Easter. Here a parish must distinguish between its mood and its conviction. Its *mood* – which has to do with feelings – may not always, even at Easter, be a confident joyful one: it may be dominated by an awareness of the absence of the kingdom in so many areas of life. However, its *conviction* – which has to do with its faith and its hope – will be one of confidence. Because it is the Church, it has faith and hope in Jesus of Nazareth. Now it contemplates the victory which God had in him. This was a victory over death – in fact a victory *through* death and *in* death. As the parish contemplates this victory, it finds in it, as well as in its own experiences of new life, a reason for hope – hope that, despite the many experiences to the contrary, God will finally be 'all in all', and Christ and his Body will, in the end, present to the Father that 'eternal and universal kingdom' of which that other Mass speaks.

Celebrating Easter
Holy Saturday itself is always a quiet day. The victory has been won, but throughout that day it is celebrated quietly and soberly – it is celebrated as, in Karl Rahner's phrase, 'a hidden victory'. This quiet celebration of the hiddenness of the victory can be consoling – it will correspond to a mood which is dominated more by a sense of the victory which has yet to be won than by a conviction about the victory which has already been won.

During the Easter Vigil, however, it is the Christian *conviction* which dictates the form and the tone of the celebration. The sure hope of the final victory of the kingdom is celebrated by the parish with unusual exuberance and with a riot of ceremony.

There is first of all the *festival of light*. Here a dark church, and a people in darkness, become slowly and gradually brightened as the light of the Risen Christ is passed from the Easter Candle to each one's personal candle. The exuberance here is such that, in a great Easter Hymn, the parish rejoices even in the evil and sin which enabled it to experience such a victory and to have such hope: 'O happy fault', it sings.

There is the *festival of story*. Here the gathered people listens again, around the Easter Candle, to the great stories of its past and, consequently of its present and its future. This really is a parish *cois teallaigh* – an evening 'around the fire' when the Christian family tells again of, and listens to, and sings about, the great events which make it the hopeful people which it is.

There is the *festival of water*, when the parish sees in the life-giving and purifying powers of water, and in its sparkling quality, a symbol of the new life which results from a life of service. Tonight, out of the womb of this water, the parish brings new members into its family.

There is the *festival of thanks*. Here the parish, in this special eucharist, praises God for assurance of the final victory of light over darkness and of life over death.

The key-word of the Easter Vigil is a cry of joy 'Alleluia'! The parish is conscious of itself as being an 'Easter People'.

Good Friday

The cross of service
Jesus did not experience the New Life of Easter without first experiencing the death of Good Friday. It was through this death that he entered into the Easter joy. On Good Friday, then, the parish focuses its attention on the Cross – that to which Jesus' life of service led him and through which his victory was achieved.

A kind of dying to oneself, a kind of death, is an essential and constant feature of every life of service – there is always self-*giving*, self-*spending* involved in service. For Jesus, the death on Calvary was not his first experience of the dying which his life of service entailed. All through his life he experienced something of this. He experienced disappointment when he was misunderstood even by disciples and friends – even by family (Mk 3:20). He experienced frustration, when he encountered unbelief and hardness of heart. He experienced loneliness and isolation, when he was rejected even by the religious leaders. It was his experience of the pain and the cost of service which enabled him to say, according to St John's gospel:

I tell you, most solemnly, unless a grain of wheat falls on the ground and dies, it remains only a single grain; but if it dies, it yields a rich harvest (12:24).

The death on Calvary was not for Jesus the beginning of dying. Rather was it 'the death of dying'.

As the parish celebrates that death to which his life of service led Jesus, it is not celebrating something which is totally foreign to its own experience. As the Body of Christ, it too will have experienced in its own life something of the pain and the sacrifice and the dying which service of the kingdom involves. It will have experienced the cost of giving, the inconvenience of foregoing comforts, the pain of listening and learning, the frustration of slow progress, disappointment at being misunderstood or misrepresented. On Good Friday, it contemplates again the fact that, in order to be an Easter People, it must also – even first – be a Good Friday people.

Celebrating Good Friday

The atmosphere in which the Good Friday liturgy is celebrated matches the aspect of service which it celebrates. The Church is stark and silent and still. The sanctuary is empty and bare.

The *Liturgy of the Word* focuses on this suffering side of service. In the first reading the prophet Isaiah's description of a servant in his moment of suffering is read. This description is, of course, extraordinarily apt in its application to Jesus. But phrases like 'through his wounds we are healed', 'ours were the sufferings he bore', 'a man of sorrows and familiar with suffering', 'a thing despised and rejected by men', must surely strike chords in the experience of the community which embodies today Jesus' service of the kingdom. So too must the reading from the Letter to the Hebrews as it speaks of the humanness and vulnerability of Jesus, of how 'during his life on earth he offered up prayer and entreaty, aloud and in silent tears', and how 'he learnt to obey through suffering'. In the reading of St John's account of the Passion, the parish hears again the story of the betrayal and crucifixion to which his life of service led Jesus.

After listening to the word, the parish venerates the Cross –'the wood of the Cross on which hung the Saviour of the world'. It is significant that, before the members of the parish do this individually, they do it together as a community. In embracing the Cross of Jesus, the parish embraces again the corresponding aspect of its own life of service, and draws strength from the Suffering Servant to endure the sufferings entailed in its own service. Its union with the 'wounded healer' is deepened in the Good Friday service of *Holy Communion*. Fittingly, the liturgy ends in silence.

Holy Thursday

Commitment

The death of Good Friday followed from Holy Thursday. Two events from the New Testament accounts of the Last Supper are remembered on Holy Thursday – 'the institution of the eucharist' and 'the washing of the feet of the disciples'. In the eucharist, I have already pointed out, Jesus symbolically expressed his commitment to service of the kingdom, 'even to accepting death, death on a cross' (Phil 2:8). Commitment to service is also what is symbolised in the washing of the feet of the disciples:

> When he had washed their feet and put on his clothes again he went back to the table. 'Do you understand,' he said, 'what I have done to you? You call me Master and Lord, and rightly; so I am. If I, then, the Lord and Master, have washed your feet, you should wash each other's feet. I have given you an example, so that you may copy what I have done to you' (Jn 13:12-5).

The close connection between the eucharist and the washing of the feet of the disciples ought to become very clear when we consider certain facts about St John's gospel. This gospel is very much a gospel of the eucharist. It is, for example, the one in which we find the great discourse on the Bread of Life (ch 6). This gospel also dwells at much greater length than any of the others on the theme of the Last Supper – five chapters are given over to this theme in St John's gospel, compared with no more than a half a chapter in each of the other three. However, despite all this, St John's gospel, alone of all four, does not give any account of what we call the institution of the eucharist. As against this, St John's gospel – again alone of the four – gives an ac-

110

count of Jesus washing the feet of his disciples during the course of the Last Supper. The close link between the two actions is that both are symbolic ways of saying:

This is myself ... at your service.

Commitment is, obviously, a constant feature of every life of service. It was a constant feature of the life of Jesus. Again and again throughout his life he had to renew his commitment to the service of the kingdom – when, for example, his family wanted 'to take charge of him' (Mk 3:20-1); when Peter wanted to stop him from facing up to Jerusalem and to the death which it meant: 'Get behind me, Satan!' (Mt 16:23); when one of his followers attempted to use violence to save him from suffering (Mt 26:51); when, in the agony scene, with the full consequences of his life of service before him, he prayed, 'Nevertheless, let it be as you, not I, would have it' (Mt 26:39). The Last Supper was not the first occasion when Jesus committed himself to service and to the suffering which was involved; it was the final symbolic expression of his commitment.

On Holy Thursday the parish celebrates this feature of Jesus' life of service, and of its own life of service too. It is reminded that commitment has to be constantly renewed. On Holy Thursday the parish focuses on the fact that it is an Easter People because it is a Holy Thursday People – a people always committing itself anew to the service of the kingdom of God.